Wiltshire

Tales of

MYSTERY & MURDER

Other counties covered in this series include:

Berkshire
Buckinghamshire
Cheshire
Cornwall
Derbyshire
Devon
East Anglia
Essex
Hampshire
Hertfordshire
Kent
Lancashire
Leicestershire
Lincolnshire
Middlesex
Northamptonshire
Nottinghamshire
Somerset
Staffordshire
Surrey
Sussex
Warwickshire

Wiltshire
·Tales of·

**MYSTERY
&MURDER**

Roger Evans

COUNTRYSIDE BOOKS
Newbury, Berkshire

COUNTRYSIDE BOOKS
3 Catherine Road
Newbury, Berkshire

To view our complete range of books,
please visit us at
www.countrysidebooks.co.uk

ISBN 1 85306 937 X
EAN 978 1 85306 937 6

Cover design by Peter Davies, Nautilus Design

Produced through MRM Associates Ltd., Reading
Printed by Arrowsmith, Bristol

Contents

MAP OF WILTSHIRE

THE MAN THEY HANGED TWICE

---❀---

The 17th century was perhaps the most violent period in the history of England. It began with the Gunpowder Plot, experienced two civil wars at its midpoint and finished with the Monmouth Rebellion. After the rebellion, many rebels were executed or deported. Others who escaped the law turned to a life of crime. Highway robbery was rife and those found guilty of such practices were hanged by the neck until dead.

Patrick O'Bryan was the son of an impoverished family who lived in County Galway, Ireland. He came to England when he enlisted into the Coldstream Guards, a position which provided a regular income, something he had never enjoyed before. But the more he had, the more he wanted to spend. Local inn and shop keepers instantly took to him and trusted him. They let him run up a tally which soon turned into an unmanageable debt. It's a familiar story and the credit was switched off. He turned on his Irish charm and borrowed from anyone kind enough to fall for his smooth talking. But eventually even those friends and acquaintances withdrew their support. It was time for Patrick to step onto the ladder of crime.

He accosted a Croydon vicar named Clewer he knew to have a bit of a record himself from many years before. In the vicar's younger days, he had stolen a silver cup and his hand had been burnt as a punishment, the scars remaining as a message to one and all. He now led a more or less honest life but still knew a trick or two. O'Bryan demanded money of him but had chosen the wrong man. He had none to give and so O'Bryan suggested he forfeit his vicar's gown. Clewer agreed as long as it was won fairly in a game of cards. The game was played and the gown changed hands.

O'Bryan stole a horse and deserted from the Guards. His days of highway robbery had begun. On one memorable occasion, he held up Nell Gwyn, a favourite of the king, Charles II. Switching on his Irish charm once again, he told Nell that, just as she had served a great many men with her favours, he likewise had satisfied a great many women; and if he could ever offer her the same service, he would be only too delighted to do so. But in the meanwhile, could she lighten her purse in his favour? She smiled at his cheek and gave him ten guineas.

As his career progressed, he kept company with young men who he found easy to corrupt and involve in his robberies. One young lad was captured the very first time he worked with O'Bryan. He was hanged at Worcester. Other associates of O'Bryan met similar fates. Inevitably, O'Bryan himself was captured, charged with highway robbery and condemned to death.

After a restless night in the cells, he was taken to the gallows. A priest walked with him reading from the bible. They ascended the steps of the gallows together. The hangman placed the noose around O'Bryan's neck, pulled the knot tight on one side and he was sent to meet his maker. After his body had hung from the gallows for the prescribed length of time, he was cut down and delivered to a group of his acquaintances who had agreed to see to his burial. It was a solemn group that carried his body to the home of one of the band. There he was laid out in the usual fashion and his friends stood in silent memory – until it appeared that his body moved. Could this simply be the nerves in the body twitching? Could it be the first twinge of rigor mortis? There were no other apparent signs of life.

It was with some difficulty that they persuaded a doctor to pay a visit to bleed him. This would have two purposes. Firstly, dead bodies don't bleed and so they would know if he was dead or simply in a deep coma. Secondly, bleeding, if done in moderation, was a recognised technique for reviving an otherwise unconscious person. Amazingly, O'Bryan recovered.

He made all those present swear to secrecy. They in turn pointed out to him that what had happened was a chance in a million and he should not waste this opportunity to change his ways and lead an honest life. They agreed to support him while he got back on his feet and they did so. He in turn followed an honest path, at least for a while but then fell back into his old habits. He stole a horse and returned to highway robbery, this time bolder than ever. Perhaps he believed that he was invincible, having already cheated the law. Perhaps he saw it as a game, him versus the law. If so, imagine how he felt when he held up a new victim only to discover him to be the very man who had convicted him at his trial.

Imagine too the shock, and then the confusion, of the judge as he saw before him the likeness of the man he had sentenced to death a year before and who he knew had gone to the gallows.

'How can this be?' challenged the shocked judge. 'You hanged twelve months ago.' 'Then I must be a ghost,' replied O'Bryan, who knew that he had to silence the judge if his survival was to be kept secret. He shot the judge through the head and then, using a large knife, dismembered the body.

Deeds of an even more dastardly nature were to follow. Lancelot Wilmot lived in a large house, a mile and a half from Trowbridge, with his wife, daughter and a handful of servants. Squire Wilmot was a man of means and it was rumoured around the county that within his walls he had a considerable fortune and much silverware. O'Bryan, now well and truly out of retirement, had acquired a small gang of villains. Having heard the rumours of Squire Wilmot's fortune, under cover of darkness they approached his home. Finding a way in was not difficult and within minutes they had bound and gagged the family servants.

Quietly they approached the bed chambers and soon found the room with the squire and his wife. In similar fashion, they too were bound and gagged. Moving on, the gang came to the daughter's room where she slept alone. She was young and tempting. Each villain in turn forced his attentions on her. She struggled and screamed, resisting with every ounce of her body as they partook of their evil pleasure. Having finished with the girl, they stabbed her for making the experience such a difficult one. Going back to the parents' room, O'Bryan said he would teach them a lesson for raising a girl who showed such resistance and such ill-manners. He stabbed them as well.

The villains searched the house and took everything of value they could carry. On leaving, they set fire to the building and all inside were consumed in the flames, including the servants, burned alive. Any evidence of the presence of the murderers was also destroyed and the world would believe that a tragic fire was the only misfortune that night.

The years passed and the gang went their separate ways. Eventually one was captured, tried and sentenced for a crime in Bedfordshire. Found guilty, he was hanged at Bedford but, before going to the gallows, he confessed all those previous sins which he could remember. They included the raid on the home of Lancelot Wilmot, in which he implicated Patrick O'Bryan. Within days, O'Bryan was seized at his London lodgings and taken to Newgate prison until the time came for his trial in Salisbury. He confessed all.

The judge, in passing the death sentence, was well aware of the murder of one of his fellow judges by O'Bryan and of O'Bryan's escape from death all those years before and was determined it would not happen again. On 30 April 1689, O'Bryan was taken to the gallows and launched into eternity. His body was then taken down and hung in chains within sight of the former home of Lancelot Wilmot, there for all to see that he did not escape a second time.

THE WITCH OF
FISHERTON ANGER

---❀---

In the 17th century Fisherton Anger was a small village, just on the edge of Salisbury, where Fisherton Road now gives a clue to its location between the railway station and city centre. It was there that an aged crone lived, called Anne Bodenham. This was a time when country folk went in fear of witchcraft and across the nation tens of thousands of women were burnt at the stake, accused of demonic crimes. Fear and superstition prevailed and anyone considered old and ugly was equally considered to have the potential to be a witch.

Anne Bodenham was 80 years old. She lived alone and made a modest living teaching youngsters to read and write. She was, in fairness, a learned lady, having worked for many years for a Dr Lambe, and probably had a reasonable understanding of natural medicines gained whilst in his service. This on its own was enough to throw suspicion on her. She was also a Catholic in very Protestant times and there was enough bigotry amongst the local Puritan folk to arouse suspicion. But it was her association with Dr Lambe which was her downfall.

Twenty five years earlier, in 1628, John Lambe had been tried and executed as a witch. He had been an advisor to George Villiers, who in turn was an advisor to both James I and Charles I. Advisors to kings inevitably have enemies. There were those who wanted Villiers out of the way but he was too popular with Charles. So they plotted to discredit Lambe, who was the easier target, and through him bring down Villiers.

Lambe was charged with 'certain evil, diabolical and execrable arts called witchcrafts, enchantments, charmers and sorcerers' and a whole string of other offences. He pleaded innocent but was found guilty. Having been sentenced to death, members of the jury began to die unexpectedly – so he was temporarily reprieved. He was then accused of raping an eleven-year-old girl, condemned to death and pardoned by the king, perhaps as a favour to Villiers. In June 1628 a mob of apprentices took the law into their own hands. They chased Lambe through the streets and beat and stoned him to death.

During those years, Anne Bodenham had been in his employment. He was keen to teach her and she was keen to learn. She read the many books in his library and familiarised herself with medicine. And perhaps that was her only real crime when, in 1653, she was accused of witchcraft. Anne was a clever woman. Clever women were considered to be cunning. Witches were cunning women. The logic was simple and she stood accused of bewitching a maid.

At her trial, highly dubious evidence was stacked up against her: if Lambe had poisoned the king, she had probably had a hand in it; she could cure diseases by charms and spells, and would say prayers that had the same effect; she could reveal the whereabouts of lost and stolen items – and took money for the privilege; she would stare into a green crystal ball in which she could show others what was happening there and then in their homes, all revealed in the glass. On another occasion, a young woman went to her, believing that two of her family wanted to poison her. Anne sent her home with a black dog to lead the way. Arriving at her home, the doors threw themselves open, clearly indicating the poison theory to be true. Later Anne visited the house and summoned Beelzebub, Satan and Lucifer to appear. A devilish wind whipped up and shook the house. The doors flew open and in walked five spirits dressed as young urchins. It doesn't have to make sense to us today but suffice it to say that all those centuries ago, such things were taken as literal and as fact.

The evidence had been given principally by only two witnesses, Edmond Bower and Anne Styles. Most of what Bower said was simply repeating what Anne Styles had told him. It was Anne who gave the evidence above, and her accusations grew in fantasy as she got deeper into them. Anne Bodenham could turn herself into a hare, toad, bull, bear, lion, wolf or a great black cat. She could put a spell on anyone such that they would fly 40 miles through the air. Women who stripped her naked in the prison, to examine her body for signs of the devil, found a mark on her shoulder about the size and with the appearance of a nipple, with which she could suckle the devil, a birthmark as we would know it today. They found a similar one near her 'secret place'. Anne Bodenham was interrogated by Bower and confessed to everything. We can only imagine the horror of that interrogation, inflicted on a frail and elderly lady of 80 years. After the death penalty had been announced, the Reverend Foster spent much time with her and reported that she actually denied all the allegations and denied ever having confessed to them.

The outcome of the trial was a foregone conclusion and Anne Bodenham was taken to Salisbury for her execution as a witch on 19 March 1653. There she called for drinks to give her courage and had to be restrained in order that she should not be drunk when she was hanged. As she walked through the streets of Salisbury, she held a small piece of silver in her hand, begging at each door for a glass of ale. Reaching the scaffold, she immediately approached the ladder and had to be held back. Clearly she now wanted to get it over, to no longer prolong the anguish. But Mr Bower wanted her sober and needed more time to get her to confess in public, so that all could hear. She refused and cursed him for holding up the proceedings. At last she climbed the steps and the hangman performed his duty. Her last words were to the hangman: 'A pox on thee. Turn me off.'

What is certain is that Anne Bodenham was an educated woman. She could hold her own in a fair argument with any man. That put her outside of the boundaries of acceptable behaviour in those days when women were expected to hold their tongues. She had worked for a man who had become a hated figure across the nation, becoming popularised as 'Dr Lambe's Darling'. She had become a target herself of hatred borne of ignorance. She was old and frail and unlikely to receive much public support. The elderly were very much viewed as a financial burden on the parish. But was she guilty of witchcraft?

Anne Bodenham conjuring up devils

What we do know is that her principal accuser, Anne Styles, had already been accused of witchcraft. It could have been Anne Styles going to the scaffold. Instead it was Anne Bodenham. When Bower had earlier extracted a confession of guilt from Anne Styles, she declared that she had not been a witch but had been affected by visits to Anne Bodenham. It was Bodenham who was the witch and who had put the spell on Anne Styles. It is easy to see that Bower now had the opportunity to rid Wiltshire of the woman who had become the hate figure. Anne Styles was spared, whether she was a witch or not, and it was Anne Bodenham who was taken to the scaffold. Whether or not you believe in witchcraft, you would expect someone to have noticed that she was a witch before she had reached her eightieth year.

JOHN GURD'S
DOUBLE MURDER

---❁---

John Gurd was born on 11 December 1861, the son of a master shoemaker in the village of Donhead St Mary near Shaftesbury. He grew up with his parents, John senior and Hannah, his two sisters, Eleanor and Mary, and a brother. When John junior was just five years old, his father died aged 44. His mother was left to bring up the young family on whatever she could earn as a dressmaker.

When he was old enough, Gurd enlisted in the Dorset Militia and from there transferred into the Dorset Regiment, serving as a regular soldier. Aspects of John Gurd's dishonesty were already beginning to show. Perhaps he deserted from the regiment, perhaps he was running away from debts. Whatever the reason, he enlisted into the Royal Marines under the false name of Louis Hamilton. He enjoyed his time with the marines but was struck down with an illness and was invalided out with a pension, still under his assumed name.

It was as Louis Hamilton that in August 1890 he applied for the position of attendant at the Wiltshire County Asylum in Devizes. He still kept the secret of his identity to himself and certainly didn't tell Florence Adams who was a housemaid at the asylum. Florence fell in love with John Gurd, or Louis as she knew him, and the two became betrothed.

The weeks passed, the wedding banns were read at St John's church in Devizes and all was set fair for the happy occasion. Both Gurd and his fiancée gave notice to the asylum that they would be leaving in a month in the hope of finding better positions. Gurd applied for a few days off to go and sort out some family business in Shaftesbury. While he was away, Florence slowly became aware that Louis was not quite the man she thought he was. One by one, those to whom Gurd owed money went to Florence, including patients in the asylum and local tradesmen, and asked when they could expect to be paid. Then Florence's uncle put paid to her plans by revealing a few home truths about her fiancé, debts here and debts there. Florence wrote to Gurd and told him that she was breaking off the engagement. Enraged, he paid her a visit and showed her a revolver, telling her that if he didn't marry her, no one else ever would. He would blow her brains out first and then shoot her 'old people', presumably a reference to her uncle and grandparents.

Gurd was furious – but who to blame first? From his point of view, Florence's uncle, Henry Richards of Melksham, was the easiest target. It was Saturday, 16 April 1892. Gurd left Shaftesbury and walked to Warminster, hoping to catch a train to Melksham. He arrived just too late for one and spent the next couple of hours in the Masons Arms, where he had a couple of pints before catching the later train. He chatted amicably to others in the inn and joined in the lively conversation in the railway carriage, showing no signs of pent up anger.

Arriving at Melksham at 8.20 in the evening, he went to the King's Arms and then to the Crown Inn where he found Henry Richards. They spent the next couple of hours in apparently friendly conversation with no signs of any argument. When time was called at 10 pm, they left together and walked towards Richards' house in Devizes Road, near the canal. A lady, Sarah Ann Gale, passed them on the way. On reaching Spa Road, Gurd pulled his revolver and shot the unsuspecting Richards in the back. He didn't fall immediately but just stood there. The lady who earlier had passed them, heard the shot and turned to see what had happened. She saw a flash as the second shot hit Richards in the back. He staggered towards her, crying 'I'm a dead man' just before he hit the ground, mortally wounded. Gurd ran as fast as he could down the Spa Road, passing a young lad on the way. Asked what the noise was, Gurd replied that it was just some lads letting off crackers.

He carried on down the Spa Road to the home of his former fiancée's grandparents. He had visited them on three or four occasions with Florence. He knocked on their door but, fortunately for them, they were sound asleep and Gurd continued on his way, escaping to Bath. There he drank in a public house until his money ran out. He would need to get closer to his home to get more cash.

Donhead St Mary church where John was baptised in December 1861

Meanwhile his victim had been carried the short distance to his house and the doctor sent for, but Richards was dead before he arrived. The police issued a description of Gurd:

Wanted. Charged with a wilful murder at Melksham,
Louis Hamilton, age 29, height 5 ft. 7 in.,
fair complexion, sandy moustache, no whiskers, thin face,
dark brown hair, rather curly or frizzy.
Dressed in a large light plaid, supposed black bowler hat,
or may be wearing dark coat and vest. A native of
Higher Coombe, Shaftesbury. May be carrying a revolver.

Gurd remained undetected until the Monday night when he arrived at Corsley, near Warminster. There the landlord of the White Hart had died the previous week. It was the day after the funeral and the landlady, Mrs Rendall, had been visited by two of her brothers-in-law, John and William, who farmed nearby and a cousin, Emanuel Rendall. The customers had gone, it being after 10 o'clock, and the doors were locked. A loud knock came at the door and they asked who was there. It was Gurd looking for a pint to drink but his responses to their questions made no sense and they refused to open the door. Then came the sound of a pistol shot. Fearing that the stranger had shot their horse, the brothers rushed outside and there they could smell the fresh gun smoke. Gurd had already disappeared into the night and they discovered that the horse was wounded, albeit not too seriously.

Emanuel left to notify the police and Constable Chandler and Sergeant Read went in search of the miscreant. From the inn they walked towards Warminster and reached the farm of a Mr Downs at Corsley Heath. Hearing a noise in the yard, the two officers stopped and listened, decided it was a pig foraging and moved on. In fact it was Gurd who, thinking the two officers would turn off to sneak up behind him, left the yard and took the road towards Warminster, the very direction in which the officers were already heading.

Meanwhile, the Rendall brothers had become increasingly concerned about the state of their horse and decided to take him to the vet in Warminster, a journey which would take them past the police station. They went in to make sure that Superintendent Perrett was aware of what was going on. He had only just got back from searching unsuccessfully for Gurd but, despite it being three in the morning, set out again immediately with Sergeant Enos Molden and Constables Langley and Davis. Molden, who had spent 29 years in the police force, was just short of his fiftieth birthday and looking forward to his retirement pension.

As the group of four headed towards Corsley, coming towards them from the other direction were the other two officers and, now ahead of them, Gurd. Close to the entrance to Longleat Park, by Whitebourne Cottage, the officers and Gurd spotted each other through the darkness. Gurd moved over to the side of the road on which the superintendent was waiting and asked if the officer was looking for himself. Perrett replied that he was, and for the murder of a man in Melksham. Gurd instantly stepped back and pulled his revolver, aiming it at the superintendent. Perrett threw himself at Gurd, wrestling him onto the bank, but not before Gurd fired two shots, one of which hit Sergeant Molden just beneath the heart. 'I'm shot,' he cried. 'Oh dear. I'm dying', and then fell into the arms of Constable Davis. Perrett and Langley seized Gurd and secured him with handcuffs. Nearby was a gamekeeper's cottage where they took the injured Molden. Within ten minutes, he was dead.

Gurd was taken to Warminster and charged with two murders. As daylight broke, the news soon went around the town that the local sergeant had been murdered. A huge crowd gathered outside the town hall, waiting to see the prisoner. The following day he was transferred in a covered carriage to Trowbridge.

At the inquest and trial, evidence was given by Florence Adams, Sarah Ann Gale, and various people that Gurd had spoken to on the train and in the public houses. Gurd pleaded guilty and said he was ready to die for his crime. He just wanted to get it over. The judge insisted that he should have a proper defence and a fair trial, which he did. With so many witnesses to each of the two murders, the verdict was inevitable. On 23 July 1892, Gurd was sentenced to death by hanging.

In his last few days, he spent much time with the prison chaplain, the Reverend A. Davis, expressing contrition for

Florence Adams and John Gurd – illustrations drawn at the time of the trial

his crimes. He wrote letters in response to those he received from his aunt, Ann Hayter. He explained to her that he had been afraid to write to her or his cousins, knowing how badly they must have thought of him. He said it was the break up of his relationship with his fiancée that had broken his heart, and that when he visited her uncle, Richards had mocked him and refused to return something that was at his house. And he asked that God should forgive him.

He slept well the night before the execution and walked confidently to the scaffold accompanied by the chaplain reading the burial service. Mr Billington, the hangman from York, set the drop at 6 feet 10 inches. On 27 July 1892, he breathed his last. At the inquest after the execution it was declared that the drop had failed to break his neck, it being so muscular. Death had been by shock as the primary cause and asphyxia as the secondary. It was a full minute and a half after the drop before he died.

THE LEYS LINES
OF WILTSHIRE

————— ✿ —————

Take an Ordnance Survey map and highlight ancient sites: standing stones, henges, tumuli, old forts, ancient churches, burial grounds, even dewponds. Cast your eye over the map and see how many can be joined up to create a straight line. You may be surprised how easy it is to find significant alignments. But is this a phenomenon with a valid explanation or is it that statistically, given enough points on the map and sufficient imagination on our own part, such alignments would happen naturally?

Let's assume that these lines are more than just coincidence, that man has had some influence. How then can we convince the sceptics that this is not just a random act of nature? Why would ancient man want to create such lines?

These lines are often referred to as ley lines and increasingly we hear of speculation that they are energy lines, reflecting the earth's natural energy, and that they even have healing powers. That is not a line down which I shall tread. I simply want to consider the most logical explanation for such lines, that they are ancient roadways, dating back thousands of years.

When we look at maps, we can often see long straight roads, such as the Fosse Way, and Iknield Street which runs into Wiltshire. We naturally assume they are Roman. But how can we then explain the long straight roads we find in Ireland where the Romans never went, or the straight lines which cross Peru for mile after mile and date back thousands of years? Many of the Roman roads as we know them pass along lines of travel which existed well before the Romans arrived. How do we account for that?

Let's begin by first looking at some of the 'travel lines' which run through Wiltshire.

The Old Sarum Line

The line illustrated below shows the approximately north to south lie of just one of many lines of travel which run through Stonehenge. It begins to the north of Stonehenge with a tumulus

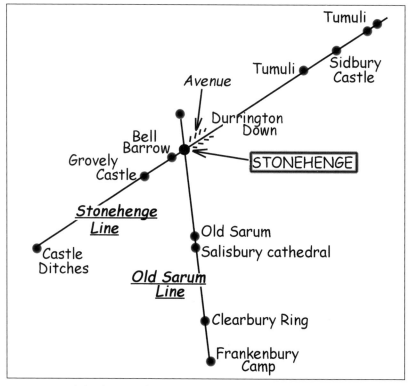

Just two of the lines which cross through Stonehenge

on Durrington Down, runs down through Stonehenge and on through Old Sarum, Salisbury Cathedral, Clearbury Ring and Frankenbury Camp, just east of Fordingbridge in Hampshire.

Old Sarum is a major earthwork enclosure. It has deep ditches indicating the need to defend an important Iron Age hill fort site, well before the Romans arrived. Salisbury Cathedral, although built in the 11th century, was almost certainly built on or adjacent to an earlier pagan religious site, as was the norm in the early days of Christianity. Clearbury Ring is another Iron Age camp. Albeit the earthworks are no longer very impressive, the trees of Clearbury Ring are visible for considerable distances, significant for the traveller. Frankenbury Camp also turns out to be an Iron Age fort.

Each of these points is a major site of historic importance and each of them is man made. The statistical chances of finding three such points in a row by coincidence is quite reasonable. Four in a row, less so. Six in a row is pushing the argument beyond the bounds of coincidence. And what if other such lines exist in the area? Can we keep arguing coincidence?

The Stonehenge Line

This and the previous line were first noted by Sir J. Norman Lockyer, the world's first professor of astronomical physics. The line runs for a distance of 22 miles from Castle Ditches through Sidbury Castle and beyond to a number of tumuli. The previous illustration shows how the Old Sarum and Stonehenge lines cross at Stonehenge.

Starting at Castle Ditches we have a hilltop earthwork. Whilst its date is unknown, it is realistic to assume it to be Iron Age. Grovely Castle is another earthwork and this one has archaeological evidence of Iron Age activity. Of particular note here is a dewpond which is on the same line and this will be mentioned again later. The bell barrow, which is part of a Bronze Age burial ground, is found near Stapleford. Next comes Stonehenge and the line, having passed through the centre of the circle, runs directly along the section of Stonehenge known as the Avenue. Next is Sidbury Castle, again an Iron Age site, followed by a number of tumuli on Cow Down.

This line gives us eight significant points and again that Iron Age link. Now eight points in a row is statistically pushing the coincidence argument into the realms of the ridiculous.

The Silbury Hill Line

Bincknoll Castle stands proud on the chalk hills with far reaching views. The benefits of its position as a defensive

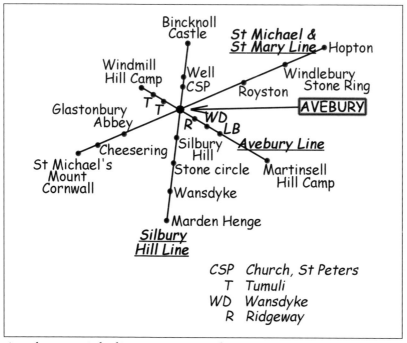

Are these straight lines mere coincidence?

site, once with a motte and bailey, are easily understood.

Travelling south from the castle, the line passes over an ancient well at Broad Hinton, then through the nearby 13th century St Peter's church. Again it is worth mentioning that this was almost certainly a religious site pre-dating Christianity. The next significant point is the stone circle at Avebury, from where it travels on to the Neolithic Silbury Hill, the largest man-made mound in Europe. Then comes a stone circle to the south of Silbury before the line crosses the Wansdyke, finally reaching the giant Marden Henge.

This line gives us another sequence of eight points, again dominated by pre-Roman activity.

The Avebury Line

Running diagonally from the north-west to the south-east, we have the Avebury line which starts at Windmill Hill Camp. Although the ditches here date back some 5,000 years, there is evidence that this was a Neolithic settlement. Travelling south, the line passes through two Bronze Age burial barrows and tumuli, before passing through Avebury Circle. It then crosses the Ridgeway, Wansdyke and a long barrow in West Woods, before reaching Martinsell Hill Camp, possibly Iron Age.

St Michael and St Mary Lines

For each of the five lines above, we have considered a start and finish point as if that is the beginning and end of the exercise. However, there is nothing to say that these lines should not reach much further, perhaps hundreds of miles across country, perhaps from coast to coast. Indeed that is the case with the St Michael and St Mary lines which run from the major landmark of St Michael's Mount on the Cornish coast to Hopton in Suffolk. These are two lines which run in close parallel between the two sites, as if they were created by starting at opposite ends of the country, now and again merging as the geography of the land dictates.

Starting at St Michael's Mount, the sites they pass through include the Cheesering in Cornwall, Glastonbury Abbey, Royston, and the Windlebury Stone Ring, finishing at Hopton in Suffolk. Bang in the centre of this line is the circle at Avebury.

Let's recap on what these so-called ley lines are. They are straight tracks which connect ancient sacred sites. You can find them all over the country and Wiltshire is so rich in major sites such as Stonehenge, where the Stonehenge and Old Sarum lines cross, and Avebury, where three of the lines mentioned above cross, that we have obvious points from which to start looking. But are they mystical? Do they have special powers? It's impossible to prove or disprove but it is safe to assume that they were 'manufactured'. If a new motorway going the entire length of the country was to be built, cutting its way through open countryside, through miles of undeveloped land, then it would be no surprise to us to discover, in 20 years' time, that there were motorway services at convenient distances along the line, industrial estates had developed along the route and housing developments likewise had sprung up around the junctions.

Nor would it surprise us if, when another motorway was built going across the breadth of the country, we found exceptional developments at the point where the motorways crossed. Now consider life thousands of years ago when most of the country was covered in trees, when there were no roads let alone motorways. But people still needed to trade and that required travel over extremely long distances.

To travel those distances in the absence of roads and signposts required a particular skill and knowledge. Five thousand years ago, people were closer to nature. They relied more heavily on the sun than we do now and used simple, natural methods. The most reliable way to navigate over a long distance was to use poles, like surveyors' poles. Imagine three men, each with a pole. Man A stands at the start of a walk with his pole held before him. Man B walks forward in the approximate direction they want to travel until he stops and holds his pole in position. Man C then walks on ahead and occasionally looks back to ensure he is in line with the poles held by A and B. Then he stops and man A goes to the front and looks back occasionally to see if he is still keeping in the straight line.

In this way those three men could travel hundreds of miles in a perfect straight line, but it would be tedious travelling. Life would be easier if, once a route had been discovered, markers could be put along the line, perhaps a clump of trees or a gap in the trees on the ridge of a hill. Such landmarks are visible at a considerable distance. Even in the half light at either end of the day, they will be seen on the horizon. Now and again, markers would be needed on the low ground as well as the high. Dewponds stand out well and reflect the moonlight. So we can see how natural markers can be manufactured along these lines of travel.

The men who had the knowledge to create these lines were seen to have power. They were held in high esteem, perhaps even worshipped. Consider the Cerne Abbas Giant in Dorset, how he has been carved in the chalk hillside and stands proudly with a pole or rod in each hand. This ancient carving surely depicts someone who had the knowledge of using rods to travel across the country, along 'rod ways', roadways.

Since these were pagan times, it is reasonable to believe that not only would waymarkers be placed along these ancient routes, but that religious and burial sites would spring up along them. How often do we find ancient churches at crossroads? Why were those executed for criminal activities so often buried at crossroads?

So there we have it. Britain was criss-crossed with travel

lines, routes which needed to be straight wherever possible, because it was the simplest and safest way to travel long distances, even where hills were in the way. Religious sites sprang up along these lines and therein lies the explanation for so many Iron Age settlements and religious sites in linear patterns with each other. We can find numerous examples of churches currently in use along these lines, and this can be explained by the practice of building 'new' churches on old pagan sites. There are certainly too many examples to be coincidence. And at the major junctions, where lines cross, we have the most magnificent sites of them all, Stonehenge and Avebury.

So one mystery is solved but another remains. There are those who believe that 'earth energies' run along these lines and that this can be proved by dowsing. There are those who believe that healing powers can be found along the lines and that UFOs use them in their navigation. I'll settle for ancient lines of travel – but who knows?

THE MOTHER
BEATEN TO DEATH

❖

From womanhood to the grave, Ann Little's life was one of deprivation and violence. She was born in 1796 in the village of Box near Bath, the daughter of James and Ann Little, and grew up with her younger sister Hester and brother James. It was a reasonable childhood but, aged fifteen, she moved to London where she spent the next six years. It was six years in which she abandoned her moral upbringing, her life taking a depraved turn. She returned to live in Kingsdown in Box, to a house described as 'the receptacle for thieves and persons of bad character, and too often of the produce of the night's plunder – sheep and lambs having often been lost by the neighbouring farmers and traced to this locality'. She hadn't been back in the neighbourhood for long before she was convicted at Warminster for stealing potatoes and sentenced to three months in prison.

In May 1817 she had her first child, an only daughter called Grenada. The father was Thomas Bullock, a watch-maker. Four years later, George was born, father unknown. In September 1826 Thomas arrived, the son of Thomas Newman, whose occupation was described as 'On His Majesty's Service'. Early in 1832 a fourth child, James, arrived, father unknown.

Some years later, she settled with the widower Isaac Smith, a quarryman who worked as a labourer on the railways. He was fifteen years younger than Ann and stood at five feet seven inches with brown and grey hair, hazel eyes and had a drinking habit, but not as bad as Ann Little's if the opinion of her neighbours is to be believed.

It was a recipe for a tormented and violent relationship. With Isaac came his two sons, fourteen-year-old William, who also worked as a quarryman, and Francis, an eleven- year-old farm labourer. Two older sons were already making their own way in life. Although Grenada was no longer living at home, Ann's three sons were still there; young George was employed as a farm labourer.

They had lived together for almost two years when Ann gave birth to their son who took his father's name of Isaac. This was Ann's fifth illegitimate child by at least the fourth father. Their address at this time was given as 'near the three firs, Kingsdown, Box.' It appears that the couple nearly got married. The banns had been published and the big day came. On their way to church, we have to assume that they stopped at the inn and by the time they had finished drinking, they had no money to pay for the ceremony.

The months passed with the couple still unmarried. It was Saturday, 4 September 1841, young Isaac was almost a year old and still 'at the breast' as the court later heard. His father had picked up his week's wages and, with his eldest son, had headed straight for the Grove Inn at Ashley, near their Box home. It was about seven o'clock in the evening. They were part way through their first pint of ale when Ann Little arrived, drunk as a lord, with the baby in her arms. Isaac's other son Francis was with her. The family group stayed until about ten o'clock by which time they had put away another four pints. Isaac had become distinctly drunk and Ann Little was in an even worse state, albeit they left the inn quietly and without causing trouble

They had begun the walk home, with young Francis carrying the baby. Isaac asked Ann for a shilling so that he could have another pint in the Swan. She refused and they continued on their way. It was approaching midnight and they were almost at the door when Isaac asked her how much money she had. We can only presume he was not impressed with her answer. Swinging a punch, he knocked her to the ground. For a while she sat on a grass bank and then ran off. Isaac and his son continued on their homeward journey.

On reaching the house, they found the door was locked and Isaac tried unsuccessfully to kick it down. He retraced his steps to find Ann and saw her walking up the road towards him. Asking her where she had been, she replied that she had been for a drink in the Swan. He asked her why she ran away. She refused to answer and he swung another punch, knocking her again to the ground. She took off one of her pattens to defend herself. A patten is a shoe mounted on a heavy metal ring to raise the wearer above a muddy surface. It makes a formidable weapon. She begged him to stop but as she started to rise, he punched her again and again until she sank to the ground once more. Then, cursing her as he did so, he laid into her with his boot in a most savage and horrific manner. 'Lord, Isaac! You have killed me,' she screamed in terror, to which he replied, 'Damn your eyes. I will kill you.' He walked on and turned to see her attempting to follow him, and struck her down once more.

Despite Ann's screams for mercy, a neighbour passed by, reluctant to get involved. Indeed many of the neighbours heard the fracas but were afraid to interfere, such was the couple's reputation. Ann lay in the road in a state of collapse and was then dragged to their house by Isaac. Eventually he picked her up only to let her fall again.

She was taken into the cottage, bleeding from a blackened eye and with blood slowly spreading across the lower part of her dress. Isaac threw her to the floor muttering, 'Bide there and die.' Soon the baby was crying with hunger and Isaac shouted that she should 'give the baby some breast'. Asked by his stepmother to do so, William passed her the baby and Francis propped Ann up as she fed the child. William meanwhile fried potatoes for his father's supper and then helped Ann into a chair. Isaac and the boys went to bed and left Ann either asleep or unconscious in the chair. And that was where young Thomas found her, unmoved, at four o'clock the following morning, cold and dead, her face and legs severely bruised. From the hips down her clothes were drenched in blood. At the back of her undergarments was a great cut. Thomas ran into his father's bedroom crying, 'Mother's dead!' 'Oh, is she?' came his almost disinterested response. He went down to see for himself and in a few minutes returned to his bed and told William that 'You'd better go and get your uncle.' He rolled over and went back to sleep.

On 5 September 1841 Mr Goldstone, the medical examiner, produced his report, and the coroner, Mr W. B. Whitmarsh, questioned some of those who had witnessed the events. Even young Thomas was called upon to testify but his evidence was rejected as insubmissable when it was realised that he was unfamiliar with the nature and purpose of the oath, never having been to chapel or church, never having learnt his catechism and having no awareness of the consequences of telling lies. To the coroner's horror, the lad had no knowledge of God or what a bible was.

Nonetheless, there was sufficient information available for the coroner to draw his conclusions. Death, primarily from three cuts, was by wilful murder and Isaac Smith would stand trial. He was committed to the new prison in Devizes pending the quarterly assizes.

On 3 March 1842, 37-year-old Isaac Smith faced his judge and jury at the Lent Assizes in Salisbury. The evidence was put forward and the jury asked to consider their verdict. The defence argued that this case was not one of murder, not even manslaughter, it was simply a case of common assault.

The judge summed up and pointed out the three options of murder, manslaughter or common assault and explained the difference between them. Murder required malice aforethought. He explained that drunkenness was no excuse in the eyes of the law. Drunk or sober, the intention is the same.

The jury returned from their deliberations and announced their verdict – guilty of murder. There then appeared to be confusion over terminology, and it worked in Isaac's favour. The judge made a comment about drunkenness not being an excuse for a crime, presumably satisfied that the jury had come to the right verdict. One of the jury, however, seemed to misunderstand what the judge had meant and said that he understood that they could not reduce the verdict from murder to manslaughter. The judge said it was their prerogative to return whatever verdict they felt was appropriate and so they re-convened, now apparently believing that the judge was strongly hinting that manslaughter was what they should have agreed. And so they did.

Instead of the death penalty, Isaac Smith was sentenced to transportation for life. He was following in his brother's footsteps, the brother already being in Australia. He was taken to the prison at Fisherton Anger, where his eldest son was already in gaol. Three weeks later he was incarcerated on the prison ship, the *Leviathan Hulk*, in Portsmouth Harbour. After five months he was transferred to the *Maitland*, a transport ship, and a six-month journey took him and 194 other convicts to Norfolk Island, Van Diemen's Land (Tasmania, as we now know it). It was where the most evil convicts were taken and the gaolers were of the toughest breed.

After two and a half years, Smith was transferred to Hobart, the capital of Tasmania. Presumably it was felt he was no longer a threat to anyone's life but his behaviour still left much to be desired. In April 1849, he was charged with misconduct in a brothel and given seven days in solitary confinement followed by hard labour. In August 1850 he was back at it again. Misrepresenting himself as a free man, he was back in the brothel and helping a man to resist arrest. Six months' hard labour in chains was the price he paid for that transgression. It was decided to transfer him to the interior, away from the nightlife of Hobart. In January 1855 he was finally granted a conditional pardon after two earlier applications had been refused. This allowed him to live in Tasmania as a free man. Still in his mid forties, he had the chance to rebuild his life. He died in Hobart in the 1870s.

Meanwhile Ann Little had been buried on 8 September 1841 in the churchyard at Box. What happened to her daughter Grenada is unknown but George and Thomas remained in Box. Isaac, Ann's youngest, died from consumption in the Lacock workhouse when just a year old. He was buried there in the churchyard. James married and moved to South Wales and worked as a miner, raising a family in the Rhondda Valley. I am indebted to his great-great-great-granddaughter, Angharad Little, for making available to me the family papers and allowing me to reveal the tragic story of her ancestor, Ann Little.

THE WILD BEASTS
OF WILTSHIRE

❁

The Beast of Bodmin Moor, the Beast of Exmoor, the Beast of Mendip and numerous others all have one thing in common. They remain unresolved mysteries which run and run just like the beasts at their centre. Wiltshire likewise has its beasts, but with a difference.

In Wiltshire there is hard evidence of the presence of wild cats, albeit in limited numbers. But there also remains the unresolved mystery of the other, bigger, wild cats which roam the countryside and if all the sightings are believed, in considerable numbers. Do they exist? Are there breeding communities of big cats out there? On Salisbury Plain and across rural Wiltshire there are plenty of small mammals, wild deer and rabbits which, if we believe the beasts exist, could provide their staple diet. In summer, when the tourists abound, they can find suitable cover away from the hordes, perhaps, in many of those restricted areas. But where did they come from?

Exotic pets

In 1976 the Exotic Pets Act was introduced. It required owners of potentially dangerous exotic species of animals to apply for a licence to keep them and to register all animals kept. Their premises were also liable to inspection to ensure the chosen species could be safely contained. For some irresponsible owners this bureaucracy was undoubtedly a step too far, or the cost of improving security was too great, and a number of exotic animals were released into the wild. Until the Act was introduced, it was neither illegal to keep wild cats nor, incredibly, to release them. Thus, in the short term, the Act had the exact opposite effect of its intended purpose with animals being released with no consideration as to their welfare nor the impact on the countryside.

So here perhaps is one explanation as to how wild cats could be wandering at large. Pumas in particular would be well suited to life in such conditions and there is no reason why this shy animal should not breed successfully in our countryside and remain unnoticed, well hidden in the dense bracken and foliage during the tourist season when its cubs would require hunting activity to be at its peak. Even at those times, it would pose no threat to humans and would do its utmost to avoid any such contact. Larger cats, such as lions, leopards and tigers would be unlikely to survive and could not go unnoticed.

Is the prospect of pumas or panthers in Wiltshire a ridiculous one? Remember that the grey squirrels which run rife in our woodlands were an introduced species. They belong to North America and the price we have paid is the loss of our red squirrels. Wallabies, porcupines, coypu, mink, and muntjac, sika and numerous other species of deer are now all so well established that many of them are classified as pests. Pumas and panthers are just more for the list.

Early records

As long ago as 1703 we can find evidence of rampaging big cats in Wiltshire, sadly from the tragic story of Hannah Twynnoy. Hannah was a 33-year-old barmaid at the White Lion Inn in Malmesbury, when a travelling menagerie came to town. It undoubtedly caused much excitement at the time.

These shows travelled the countryside with dancing bears, monkeys, occasionally a camel but rarely a lion or tiger. This one had a tiger as the star of its collection. It appears that on 23 October, the tiger escaped and local legend has it that it headed straight for the White Lion and there mauled poor Hannah to death. Another version is that Hannah got too close to the cage and was pulled inside.

Whatever the truth of her demise, the evidence is clear that it was a tiger that killed her. The headstone on her grave in the grounds of Malmesbury Abbey relates the tale in the form of a poem:

> In bloom of Life
> She's snatched from hence,
> She had not room
> To make defence:
> For Tyger fierce
> Took Life away,
> And here she lies
> In a bed of Clay,
> Until the Resurrection Day.

Hannah's experience was not the only time a big cat was loose in Wiltshire. If today you take the Andover road from Salisbury, at the village of Winterslow you will come across the Pheasant Inn. It was formerly known as the Winterslow Hut and was a favourite haunt of the essayist William Hazlitt. But it gained fame for a very different incident on 20 October 1816.

The landlord of the inn was waiting for the Exeter to London Royal Mail coach to arrive. He had already heard the sound of the guardsman's coach horn as they drew near to the inn. The coachman was just taking the pace off the horses, ready to pull into the yard of the inn, when he saw a largish animal rapidly approaching from his right-hand side and gaining ground on the coach. Suddenly it was running alongside and drew level with the horses. Too late the coachman realised it was a lioness and it was on the brink of attacking the right-hand horse of the leading pair, a horse named Pomegranate. She kicked out as best she could within the constraints of the shafts but the lioness was already tearing into her side, gouging out wounds which would leave long-lasting scars.

The coach pulled to a halt with the passengers screaming

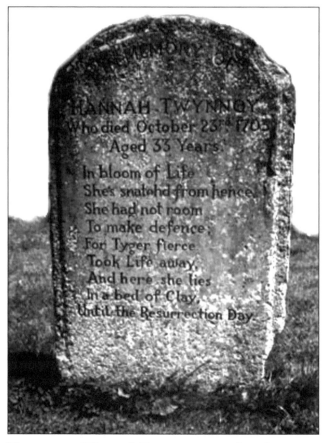

The grave of Hannah Twynnoy at Malmesbury

in terror. The guard, who had already drawn his blunderbuss, raised the weapon ready to fire when he heard desperate cries of, 'Don't shoot! Don't shoot!' The tables were rapidly turned on the lioness as an enormous mastiff tore into her, grabbing her by the leg. She immediately fought back, giving the coach and the horses time to pull away from danger.

The man crying 'Don't shoot' was the owner of a travelling menagerie. He called the dog off and spoke soothingly to the lioness. She calmed down sufficiently to walk off in a huff towards a wooden granary, which was mounted on stone mushroom-shaped stands which kept the corn raised off the ground and provided space for the lioness's safe retreat. Beneath this she took shelter and showed no resistance as her keepers calmly tethered her legs and dragged her out. Lifted onto a farmer's cart, she was taken back to the travelling caravan which continued on its journey to Salisbury Fair.

Meanwhile, the passengers made a quick dash for the safety of the inn while the guard and driver stood vigil and the horses were tended by the inn's ostler. Pomegranate was not fit to continue her journey and was exchanged for a fresh horse. Before leaving, the passengers took time to eat, drink and settle their nerves, reflecting on their adventure, which would prove to be a party piece for the telling in many years to come. But for some of the group, having a story to tell was insufficient compensation for their moment of terror. They wanted the lioness's owner punished. No sooner had they reached Andover then they gave a full report to the local press and sent a message to the magistrate at Salisbury. He called the lioness's owner before his bench and warned him to ensure his animals were kept under proper control. He also ordered that compensation should be paid to the owner of Pomegranate who, allegedly, was never the same again.

Modern times

The above incidents both related to escapees from menageries and mysterious modern day sightings cannot be so easily explained.

In the summer of 1996, a wild cat was run over by a car and killed at Black Dog crossroads near Warminster. Its body, having been taken to Paignton Zoo, was identified as that of a jungle cat (*Felis Chaus*) and can now be seen in the Westbury Museum. The jungle cat is similar to the serval and in the wild is found in Egypt, South East Asia and across the whole of India. They can weigh up to 16 kilos and have long legs with a slender build. Generally brownish in colour, their ears are tufted. They are frequently seen in daylight hours, compared to some wild cats such as panthers which prefer the cover of darkness. They feed on rodents and small mammals, even small deer, but are unlikely to take sheep or lambs. Twenty years before this incident, two jungle cats had escaped in this same area, albeit they were later reported as having been shot. Is it possible that this was one of their offspring?

In May 1998, there were three reports of puma or panther sightings in a three-week period, all in the Vale of Pewsey area and close to West Lavington. Three months later a woman reported seeing a panther in front of her car between Pewsey and Bottlesford.

During 2000, there were reported sightings of panthers and black leopards at Lavington, Trowbridge, Roundway Hill near Devizes, Devizes, Bradford Leigh, Southay in Bratton, Studley Green estate near Trowbridge, Little Cheverell, Great Cheverell and many others. In December of that year, two teenage girls reported what they believed to be a lynx cross their path at Drews Pond Lane in Devizes. This was just one of many sightings of the cat, described as having long legs and tufted ears. Just days later, a dog was attacked at its home in Coulston near Erlestoke by an animal suspected of being a leopard.

In March 2001, the landlord of a public house was travelling through Wingfield in West Wiltshire when he saw what looked to him like a panther, stalking across a field and carrying a young cub in its mouth. Large and black, it was about the size of a labrador but feline in shape and movement. Towards the end of April, a black cat-like animal, again labrador-sized and with a long tail, was seen by a couple in Low Road at Little Cheverell. It is believed it was a black leopard.

In June 2001 a married couple were walking from Yatesbury to Berwick Bassett along a footpath when they spotted a big cat some 400 yards away. They described it as the size of an alsatian and heavily built. Its back and sides were brown in colour, lightening to a tan on the under parts and legs. Its movements were quite unlike those of a dog, being the low slung, slinky cat-like movement. To these we can add more sightings in 2002 at Rowden Hill, Chippenham and Great Bedwyn, again a black panther-like creature being described.

So do these beasts exist? Are the reported sightings actually the offspring of released exotic species now turned feral? Unlike other counties, Wiltshire at least has some solid evidence of the presence of wild cats. We have clear evidence of escaped jungle cats and forensic evidence of a road kill of a jungle cat 20 years later. We have scores of reports of panther-sized cats, even some carrying cubs in their mouths. There are now a number of plaster casts taken from the tracks of these animals and identified as cats rather than dogs. Every year there are sightings reported of wild cats and the number of sightings increases with each year that passes. But still there are those who won't believe in their existence. Until someone produces another body or a well-defined photograph, the mystery continues.

WHEN LIFE SHOULD MEAN LIFE

———————⬡———————

Murder is always abhorrent but is particularly repulsive when the victim is a young child. Add to that the possibility that the child was sexually molested and it is understandable how those close to the victim can call for the re-introduction of the death penalty or at least that a life sentence should be just that, imprisonment for life. How can such a person be released back into society? This then has to be balanced against the possibility that an innocent person could hang. There are more than enough cases from the not too distant past where such miscarriages have occurred. The murder of Zoë Evans raised these questions once again.

Zoë was a slim, dark-haired, bright and happy nine-year-old girl. That's how her friends and the teachers remembered her at New Close Primary School in her home town of Warminster. She lived in army married quarters in Pepper Place with her mother, 28-year-old Paula Hamilton and her step-father, Miles Evans, a dark-haired 23-year-old driver in the Royal Logistics Corp. Paula and Miles had been married just over five months when Zoë was murdered. Her mother shortly after reverted to her maiden name.

What led Miles Evans to murder Zoë may never be known. Perhaps it was sexually motivated. Whatever the reason it appears that Miles Evans took the young girl from her bed where her mother had tucked her in, pushed a crop-top T-shirt into her mouth to stop her screams, punched

*Zoë Evans; (photo courtesy of her
grandmother Ann Hamilton)*

and beat her to a state of unconsciousness and then
suffocated her. That was the conclusion of the forensic
scientists. Detectives later investigating the case raised the
possibility of a sexual assault but, as we will realise as the
story unfolds, it was impossible to produce any forensic
evidence to corroborate that line of reasoning.

It appears that having murdered her, Evans then took her
body and buried it in a shallow grave. He used a badger sett
for the purpose, on Battlesbury Hill about half a mile from
their home.

The following morning, 11 January 1997, it was realised
that Zoë was missing. Her disappearance triggered what was

to become the largest police search ever in Britain for a missing child, costing over £1,000,000. A few days after the young girl's disappearance, Miles Evans even appeared at a news conference to make an emotional appeal for Zoë's safe return, claiming that he loved her as his own.

Six weeks after Zoë's disappearance, a Ministry of Defence police officer discovered her naked and decomposing body in the badger sett in the nearby woodland. Pathologists examining her body were later able to identify asphyxiation as the cause of death but were unable to form an opinion as to whether or not she had been sexually assaulted, such was the state of decomposition of her body. Nearby was found a blood-stained T-shirt belonging to Miles Evans. The blood was identified as Zoë's and the police focus turned to him as the prime suspect.

In April 1998, after a 14-day trial at Bristol Crown Court, Miles Evans was convicted of Zoë's murder and sentenced to life imprisonment. He showed no emotion as the jury returned its majority verdict, two members failing to agree with the others. At a press conference after the trial, an emotional Paula Hamilton attempted to read a brief prepared statement but was unable to control her emotions. A female police liaison officer stepped to her assistance and finished the statement. 'Today Miles Evans was convicted of the murder of my beloved daughter Zoë. At this time I cannot help but think that the only suitable punishment for taking the life of such a beautiful girl should be the death penalty. Only he knows the suffering he has caused and may it remain with him and burden him for the rest of his life.'[1]

The following year, at the Appeal Court in London, Miles Evans commenced his appeal against the conviction. Evans's QC told the hearing that the case against his client was based

---

[1] Source: United Press International

purely on circumstantial evidence. He also submitted that there was another potential suspect worthy of investigation and that there was evidence not presented at the first hearing. Lord Justice May concluded by stating that their lordships had reached the clear conclusion that the conviction was safe. Zoë's family breathed a collective sigh of relief.

Evans had always denied killing the girl. The evidence which had not come out in the original trial was related to the sightings of two youngsters around the time of Zoë's disappearance and the circumstances surrounding the search for the girl's body. When the police searched for Zoë, they apparently covered the area of woodland where she was eventually found. Police dogs trained in searching for bodies were brought in by the Metropolitan Police and failed to find her. It could therefore be argued that her body was not there at the time of the search but was put there only a matter of days before its discovery. By that time the police and the world's press were aware of all of Evans's movements and hence his whereabouts could be accounted for at any time during which the body could have been moved. The prosecution's counter to this was that the body had been buried deep enough to avoid detection and had subsequently been unearthed by animals.

It also came to light that two youths were seen behaving suspiciously in the area on the night that Zoë disappeared. They were later accused of raping a woman on the same evening. One, who already had a conviction for assault, denied knowing Zoë, but later changed his story when it was revealed that Zoë was a school friend of the youth's sister. Two witnesses had also been found who apparently saw two men, one of whom was hiding a bin liner in bushes whilst the other was furtively keeping watch. It was the morning following Zoë's disappearance. One fitted the description of the two youths previously mentioned. The police, having been notified, searched but found nothing. Days later, one of the youths was back, again putting something into the same place. The jury at the trial of Miles Evans had never been made aware of this possibly critical evidence in Miles Evans's defence.

Five years after the conviction of Miles Evans, the family and friends of Zoë Evans were angrily still waiting to hear just what his life sentence would mean. The news they wanted was that a minimum length of imprisonment had been specified, but none had. Zoë's grandmother was appealing for a 50-year sentence but the response from the Home Office was a letter explaining why a minimum sentence was not possible. The local press supported the campaign and hundreds of Wiltshire residents added their names to the appeal. Taxi drivers, supermarkets, local businesses, neighbours and friends all joined the campaign. In the House of Commons, the MP for Westbury, Dr Andrew Murrison, presented the petition to David Blunkett, the Home Secretary.

The anguish for the family of not knowing when Miles Evans might be released can only be imagined, fearing that at any time he could be back in society. They need to know that wasn't going to happen, to bring a closure to one part of their lives.

Consider the brutality of the murder. Stripped naked, possibly sexually assaulted, clothing shoved into her mouth to silence the screams, beaten into unconsciousness and suffocated. That is what happened to an innocent nine-year-old, bright and cheerful schoolgirl. Should a person capable of such barbarity ever be allowed to walk the streets again in a free society? It is a strong argument for life to mean life when sentence is passed, and not to mean release in seven years to possibly re-offend as we know has happened in many other cases. At the time of writing, despite petitions and questions in the House, no minimum tariff, i.e. minimum length of sentence, has been set on Miles Evans.

Zoë's mother had also called for the death penalty and here we must take a step back. Perhaps we would all feel the same if such a tragedy happened in our own homes. But consider the element of doubt which has been raised over this case by the suspicious behaviour of two youths on the same night as Zoë's disappearance. Consider also the case of Timothy Evans, the surname being purely coincidental, who was hanged in March 1950 for the murder of his daughter at 10 Rillington Place. Years after his execution, six more bodies were discovered in the house. The landlord, John Christie, who had provided evidence to help convict Timothy Evans, confessed to and was found guilty of their murder. Christie himself was hanged in July 1953. In hanging Timothy Evans, they had hanged an innocent man and in 1966 he was granted a posthumous pardon. It's a powerful argument against the death penalty, but perhaps life should still mean life.

THE MYSTERY OF
THE NAKED HIGHWAYMEN

---❀---

Imagine you're driving home. It's dark and you're on a remote country road. Ahead in the darkness, you see a car with its bonnet up and from over the top of the car you see the distraught owner waving to you, beckoning you to stop. Not wishing to leave anyone stranded in such a lonely place, you pull in dutifully to offer assistance. But it's an ambush. You are held up and robbed. You call the police and issue a description of your assailants. The police smile as they recognise the modus operandi of this gang of robbers and an identification parade is arranged. You stand behind the glass on the other side of which are eight men who all more or less fit the description you provided. Each is wearing a pair of riding boots and a mask which covers the eyes. Apart from that, they are wearing nothing but a smile!

Could you recognise the guilty party? That was exactly how the Cherhill Gang escaped detection. Who were the members? That is the mystery.

Cherhill is a village just east of Calne, an old woollen town on the River Marden which once served as a staging post on the route from Bath to London. It was on the Downs above Cherhill that the gang most frequently preyed upon their victims in the stage coaches along the Great West Road. Today the Downs are crisscrossed by footpaths and bridleways which in earlier times provided useful routes for highwaymen and smugglers. In the late 18th century, and through to the early

19th, the Cherhill Gang terrorised the locality. The law seemed unable to touch them. A gibbet with a skeleton in chains, the remains of another highwayman, did nothing to deter them. Whilst other villains had short-lived careers, the Cherhill Gang survived. So what made this group of desperados so elusive?

They had an unusual technique which made them impossible to identify. They did it naked – all except for riding boots and a mask. Their reasoning was that the majority of highwaymen were captured because they fitted the description of their clothes. 'He was average build, normal height, nothing unusual about him,' was a common description of a highwayman. But asked what he was wearing, the response would be very detailed: 'He had a green cloak with a copper coloured clasp, black boots with a broken lace . . .'

Their theory worked. Whilst most of the gang remained hidden, the one whose role was to collect the bounty would leap out in front of his victims – starkers. Except for his boots and mask, there was very little left to describe, and what was visible during the hold up would be covered up at any other time, such as when the hue and cry was raised. So their identity remains a mystery to this day.

Another attempt at disguise from a Wiltshire highway robber came in 1779 when Mrs Thring, who lived at North Burcombe, was waylaid as she walked along the turnpike road near Wilton. The highwayman approached riding a good strong horse, wielding a pistol and with further weapons tucked in his belt, primed and ready to fire. Mrs Thring was no match for such a desperado and readily responded to the highwayman's demands. Two shillings and a cloak were passed over but the robber demanded more. Her jewellery was next on the list. Just then Mrs Thring announced she could see her husband coming and the villain rode off.

Back at her home, she raised the hue and cry and a party of locals went off in search of the highwayman. Tracking him down was fairly easy, he clearly lacked experience and left an easy set of tracks to follow. The search party, reaching the end of the trail, soon arrived at the neighbouring village of Baverstock. The trail led to the house of Mary Sandall, and there in her rooms were the highwayman's clothes. Mrs Thring's aggressor had been 23-year-old Mary Sandall disguised as a man.

Mary was taken to Fisherton gaol where she was held until her trial at the Devizes Assizes. She was found guilty and sentenced to death, but was later reprieved.

Other highwaymen weren't as lucky as Mary. Mostly they ended their careers, often very short careers, on the gallows. A highwayman called Biss was born in Shaftesbury. When he was eventually captured, he admitted his guilt but appealed for clemency, arguing that he had never done anyone any harm but had only robbed the rich and helped the poor. His appeal was later put into the form of a ballad as the following single verse demonstrates:

What say you now my honoured Lord,
    what harm was there in this?
Rich wealthy Misers was abhorred
    by brave free-hearted *Biss*.
I never robbed nor wronged the Poor,
    as well it doth appear;
Be pleased to favour me therefore,
    and be not too severe.

Perhaps the judge was not a lover of poetry, for he sentenced Biss and he was hanged at Salisbury in March 1695.

Not all careers were brief. William Davies, a farmer, came from across the border in Gloucestershire. He was known as the Golden Farmer because he always paid his bills in gold. But where did the gold come from? For 40 years this man kept his second occupation secret, that of highwayman. Not even his wife knew. She thought he was off doing business. Throughout that time Salisbury Plain was a favourite patch and many a purse of gold was lifted, but never jewellery. Perhaps that was the secret of his success. Jewellery was easy to trace. Gold was not and he simply laundered it through his farming business by paying all his bills in gold dust or nuggets, and there were plenty of bills with eighteen children in his family! In 1690, aged 64, his luck ran out and he was shot during a hold up.

Wiltshire's best known highwayman was Thomas Boulter, known as the Flying Highwayman. Prior to Thomas Boulter, the village of Poulshot, to the west of Devizes, was most famous as the home of Isaac Walton, author of *The Compleat Angler*. What a contrast between the gentleman with a rod waiting patiently on the banks of a river and the

Highwaymen are often depicted as rather romantic figures by artists.

desperate highwayman instilling fear into all who crossed his path.

Boulter's father was the local miller but the son was not to follow the trade. His father was accused of stealing a horse at Trowbridge and was transported for fourteen years. Even his mother was a well known local offender, having been publicly flogged in the market place at Devizes. Not surprisingly, Thomas himself turned to crime and in 1775 held up and robbed the Salisbury stagecoach. His career as a highwayman had begun. Stagecoaches, farmers, traders, merchants, and anyone who looked as though they were worth a bob or two, were prey for Boulter. But Boulter also had a soft streak. When a lady burst into tears at the loss of her jewellery, he returned it, and a farmer whose watch had sentimental value was allowed to keep his timepiece.

Perhaps Dick Turpin served as a role model for Boulter. In many ways, Boulter's reputation followed that of the most famous highwayman of them all. He even went to Erlestoke and there he stole a horse belonging to Peter Deime – its name coincidentally was Black Bess. He embarked on a 'Dick Turpin' pilgrimage, travelling the route Turpin took to York. He had only got as far as Middlesex, where he held up numerous coaches, when he was nearly captured and had to flee for his life, back to Wiltshire and the familiar territory around Poulshot. Allegedly he stopped at several locations during his dash for his home county, both his horse and himself drinking a bottle of wine at each stop. Their dash became a crawl.

He knew it was only a matter of time before the law caught up with him and so he headed to the coast to make his way to France and freedom. His luck ran out and in July 1778 he was captured. The following month, aged 30, he was executed at Winchester. Before he died, he asked that his diaries should be published, He was proud of the fact that he had never hurt anyone, never even retaliated when being shot at.

In Wiltshire, Boulter remained a hero. He had always cut a dashing figure, this well-dressed, blond-haired, handsome man. Next to Dick Turpin, he was perhaps the best known of the nation's highwaymen. His name was on the lips of every parent – 'Look out or old Boulter will get you'. Undoubtedly his diaries added to the richness of stories of his daring-do adventures and narrow escapes and helped to create the image of a folk hero.

Boulter, Biss and Sandall, Wiltshire's highwaymen and woman. They were all captured. They were all punished. But still we are left with that mystery. Whatever happened to the Cherhill Gang and just who were they? I suspect we will never know.

MURDEROUS HUSBANDS

———————— ❀ ————————

A ghostly visitation dating back to the days of the Civil War occurs at the Red Lion at Avebury, the only inn anywhere in the world situated within a stone circle.

The inn dates back to the early 17th century when it was built as a farmhouse. The days of the Civil War came and a young man who lived there went off to do his duty as a soldier, leaving his wife Florrie at home. Florrie, alas, was a somewhat wayward young woman, for when her husband was away, she entertained her lover. To her total surprise, her husband returned unexpectedly and she was caught in 'close liaison' with the interloper. Her husband's reaction was predictable and in a furious rage, he shot the rival for his wife's affections and then slit Florrie's throat. Covered in blood, he dragged her body to the well, threw it down inside and then covered the well with a huge boulder.

Years later, around 1800, the house became a coaching inn, which we now know as the Red Lion. In the front room is the well, today with a glass cover. On occasions, visitors will get a glimpse of Florrie, dressed all in black, as she wanders the inn searching, it is believed, for a man with a beard. Why a beard? Well, occasionally a ghost described that way is also seen, so perhaps we can assume him to be the murdered lover. And what about the spectral stage coach which occasionally crosses the courtyard of the inn? Could that be her husband returning looking to repeat his act of vengeance?

Florrie and her lover were not the only Wiltshire victims of a crime of passion by a murderous husband. At Longleat, in the early 18th century, Lady Louisa Carteret married Thomas, 2nd Viscount Weymouth. She was young, beautiful, even angelic. He was not so young and was ill-tempered, prone to violent outbursts. A son and heir was born of the union but it was not a marriage blessed in heaven. What made matters worse was that Louisa, on marrying the viscount, had brought her own footman with her. He was young and handsome. There were suspicions that there was more than a mistress and servant relationship between Lady Louisa and her employee. Some say that Viscount Weymouth actually caught them in the act; others say that it was suggested to him that the relationship had simply become far too friendly. Whatever the cause, the problem was sorted, permanently. The viscount had the footman ambushed as he left the library and he was thrown down a spiral stairway. His neck was broken and he lay dead.

Fearing an investigation, the footman's body was taken to the basement where it was buried beneath the flagstone floor and the household were notified that the footman had announced his departure. Louisa didn't believe a word of it. No doubt she was fully aware of how her husband had behaved but was perhaps too afraid to implicate him. Broken hearted, she died shortly after and the Viscount left Longleat to take up residence elsewhere. Was it simply his conscience which caused him to leave or was he driven out by some unnatural force? Perhaps so, for the ghost of Lady Louisa still haunts the top passage after nightfall, looking for her loyal servant.

For those who doubt the validity of such stories, there is an interesting and relatively recent twist to this tale. At the turn of the last century, it was decided to install central heating at Longleat. A new boiler was required but there was insufficient depth in the basement to take the required size.

The only solution was to take up the flagstone floor and dig deeper down. To their surprise, there beneath the stones lay buried the skeletal remains of a man. Remnants of his clothing and the boots he was still wearing were identified as belonging to the period of Queen Anne. The remains were scooped up and taken in a box to the nearby cemetery where they were conveniently buried without the police needing to get involved.

Perhaps the most tragic tale of a murderous husband comes from Devizes Castle. Richard II of England was married to the young Isabella of Valois whilst she was still only nine years old. It appears that despite her tender years, she was suspected of falling in love with another. King Richard's barbaric solution was to have his young wife bricked up in the walls of the castle. The fear which that young child must have experienced is unimaginable. Encased alive in a brick tomb, she was left to starve to death, die of thirst or simply to suffocate. Is it any wonder that Isabella's ghost is seen pacing the corridors at the very spot where she suffered that horrific fate. At least she is not alone, for it is told that a young cavalier, complete with plumed hat, moustache and beard, wearing a fine sword at his side, also walks the corridors of the house.

Another wife starved to death by her husband was Ann Tucker, who lived in Bradford-upon-Avon. She was married to Samuel Tucker, 25 years younger than herself. Perhaps the age difference proved too great, for Samuel became determined to rid himself of her on a permanent basis. But this was to be no quick death, no bullet or sharp blade, but a long, slow, lingering and painful death.

It was 1811 and from New Year's Day until 8 March, no one was allowed to visit Ann Tucker. He kept her locked up and away from the prying eyes of the world. Meanwhile he went about his business which, although he had begun life as a weaver, was by then as a doctor of sorts. When Samuel's work took him away for a few days, he would lock his wife in a windowless room with no food or water. Unable to leave her prison, her excrement lingered unattended, creating a putrid atmosphere. Undoubtedly he knew what he was doing. Weakened by starvation and in such squalid conditions, she would be fatally prone to any illness which came her way. So he fed her with just enough to keep her alive, but only just. A small portion of potato, a little barley bread and a splash or two of water. Even the most depraved of prisoners fared better than this.

Totally emaciated through malnutrition, and unable to move, on 8 March 1811 her suffering came to an end. An enquiry into her death was called for and her corpse was examined by an independent surgeon. He described her as just skin and bone. Samuel Tucker was accused of her murder and was tried at Salisbury on 31 July. His explanation to the jury for his wife's condition was that she had a bowel disorder and despite an insatiable appetite had wasted away. He was found guilty and the judge, in announcing the death penalty, described the murder as one of the most atrocious kind.

The following day, knowing he would meet his maker on the next, he confessed his guilt to his priest. On 2 August 1811 he was executed at Salisbury and his body delivered to a surgeon for dissection.

Equally brutal, but not so prolonged was the murder of 44-year-old Emily Purcell. She lived with her husband in Bradford-upon-Avon, but it was not a happy marriage. Barely a week went by when he did not argue with her, even over the most trivial of matters. His temper was violent and the threat of some dastardly deed was ever present.

Matters came to a head on 9 November 1889. Emily had been shopping and was well pleased with the pretty floral petticoat she had bought herself. His reaction was not what she expected. Instead of complimenting her on her choice, the 50-year-old Benjamin instantly flew into a rage. Perhaps unaware of what he was doing, he grabbed an axe, swung it over his head and brought it crashing down, splitting Emily's head wide open. As if that wasn't enough, in a fit of uncontrolled fury, he viciously beat her already lifeless body with the blunt end of the axe head.

Leaning over her body, he ensured she was dead. There was no doubt whatsoever. Putting down the axe, he left the house and walked to the police station where he confessed to his horrific crime. His trial at the Wiltshire Assizes, under Baron Pollock, was a matter of formality. Purcell was found guilty of murder and sentenced to death. On 9 December 1899 at Devizes, James Berry, the hangman, carried out the execution.

THE FIFTY YEAR MYSTERY
OF PORTON DOWN

---------- ❀ ----------

It depends on how you look at it. His life was sacrificed for the sake of 15 shillings, if you see it from the victim's point of view. It was sacrificed in the interests of mankind from the scientists' point of view. But the real mystery is why it took 50 years for the truth to be told concerning the death of a young RAF serviceman. And to what other facts are the public still denied access? Porton Down holds many secrets which remain a mystery to the rest of the world.

Twenty-year-old Leading Aircraftsman Ronald Maddison, a Swindon-based RAF engineer, had been conscripted to do two years national service. In May 1953 he was one of many volunteers who agreed to be guinea pigs in experiments which, they were led to believe, were to find a cure for the common cold. A poster at his air base, calling for volunteers, had encouraged many men to step forward. He accepted the offer of the 15 shillings (75p) inducement and put his trust in the scientists at the top secret Porton Down establishment. Perhaps his real incentive was that for a few days he would be away from the boredom of service life in hutted camps where there was little to do bar watch the rain. Perhaps it was to buy an engagement ring for the girlfriend he would never see again.

He was told he would come to no harm. That proved to be far from the truth. What he was not told was that he was to be exposed to the deadly Sarin nerve gas. When a few years ago terrorists targeted the Japanese underground train system, it was Sarin gas which they used. It is perhaps the easiest deadly agent to produce.

Porton Down had been set up as a research centre on the edge of Salisbury Plain in 1916. Its purpose was to catch up with the Germans in the production of chemical weapons such as chlorine, phosgene and mustard gas. They began researching the possibilities of biological weapons during the Second World War. At the same time, Nazi scientists had discovered Sarin and another chemical nerve agent, Tabun. Britain, the USA and Canada had agreed to work together to develop these agents to have an offensive capability.

Porton Down's priorities switched from biological to chemical weapons. They already knew that Sarin caused paralysis, convulsion and severe respiratory problems. What they needed to establish was the lethal dose, the level at which at least half of those infected were killed. Two days before Ronald became a guinea pig in the trials, two other volunteers suffered serious reactions to the dosage with which they were treated. They were not the only ones and years later, hundreds of ex-servicemen were blaming the treatment they received for their serious health problems. Despite the obvious and immediate adverse effect the nerve gas was having on the volunteers, the experiments continued. Hundreds, if not thousands, were given the treatment at various levels of dosage.

At 10 am on 6 May 1953, Ronald and five other servicemen were taken one by one into a sealed chamber, each of them wearing a respirator. A layer of serge and flannel had already been taped to one arm of each man. A scientist entered the room and visiting each man in turn, dropped 200 mg of Sarin onto the piece of material. Ronald watched as the first three men were treated and then the scientist took his arm and administered the required dosage. The final two were treated and they were left alone, still with their masks on, to play noughts and crosses. The scientists observed their reactions, looking for symptoms of the nervous system being effected.

Ronald was the first to show signs of distress, within 23 minutes of being treated. He said he felt unwell and slumped forward in his chair. He was soon taken outside where he broke into a sweat and found difficulty in breathing. An antidote was applied but his condition worsened. Loss of hearing was followed by loss of consciousness. The ambulance arrived and the nineteen-year-old driver watched in horror as Ronald writhed in agony, spewing a glutinous foam from his mouth, convulsing as though electrified. Quickly the driver rushed him to the medical unit at Porton. There the other patients had already been cleared out and a group of white coated men stood waiting around a bed. The ambulanceman carried Ronald to the bed and watched as Ronald's leg rose eerily from the bed and his skin turned blue from the foot upwards. Ronald was given oxygen and adrenalin but never recovered. In just over an hour from entering the chamber, he was dead.

The following day, every room in the building smelt of strong disinfectant. The ambulance driver was recalled and instructed to take the body to a hospital mortuary and to say nothing of what he had witnessed.

The news of his son's death was broken to John Maddison. The Ministry of Defence offered £3 towards the funeral expenses. Not surprisingly, John Maddison turned down their offer of charity. An inquest was held under a veil of secrecy at Porton Down, the outcome being 'death by misadventure', and perhaps it is here that the mystery begins. The Ministry of Defence claimed that all the men who took part in the experiments had been told beforehand that they would be taking part in experiments using nerve gas. If Ronald had died after privately experimenting with drugs, a verdict of misadventure would be acceptable. If he died after being told he would come to no harm and that it was an experiment to find a cure for the common cold, and he was then treated with a deadly nerve gas, then unlawful killing is the only acceptable conclusion.

The coroner's report was never released. John Maddison was the only member of the family allowed to attend and he was sworn to secrecy, not even allowed to tell his wife of what he heard at the inquest. But what he did hear, he never accepted.

He visited the base to find out more but was excluded from the truth. A document held by the military states that John Maddison, in the interest of national security, had agreed to state that his son's death was an unfortunate accident. This conflicted considerably with John Maddison's own account.

Ronald's family never gave up seeking the truth. What happened on that day, and the circumstances surrounding it, was declared by Churchill's post-war government to be a state secret, the exposure of which would be against the interests of national security. But Ronald's family argued that he had been tricked into the experiment. Later, other servicemen stepped forward and spoke about their own experiences, how they also had been told it was a cure for the common cold that was being sought. Theirs was a powerful argument. Having formed themselves into a veterans' group, they asked the question, 'Who could believe that thousands of men would have volunteered, as they did, if the posters had mentioned nerve gas?' Relatives of others who had suffered came forward to add to the cause.

At the end of an intensive campaign, the sheer weight of evidence building up was such that in 1999 the Wiltshire Police had to respond and Operation Antler was set up to attempt to establish the truth. In the course of that operation, over 700 ex-servicemen and family members were interviewed. The enquiries were to last for four years at the end of which sufficient evidence had been gathered to justify taking eight cases forward for consideration by the Crown Prosecution Service. As the result of their findings, in 2002 Lord Chief Justice Woolf overturned the original verdict and, in what was a highly unusual occurrence, ordered a second inquest into the death of Ronald Maddison.

Prior to the start of the second inquest, it was announced that, perhaps in the interest of establishing the truth, no scientists would face prosecution. Scheduled to last for eight weeks, it began in early May 2004 with the jury being sworn in and the coroner giving his opening address. Despite the gap of half a century, evidence was taken at the Trowbridge-based hearing from some 50 witnesses, including incredibly two who were in the chamber with Ronald on that fateful day. Even the ambulance driver came forward to finally exorcise his demons. For 50 years the images of Ronald's death had haunted him, and for 50 years he had maintained his silence, afraid he would be imprisoned if he spoke of what he had witnessed on that day. The jury of six men and four women heard how ten days before Ronald's death, another man, John Kelly, had nearly died from the same treatment, a fact which was apparently never presented at the original inquest.

The result of the new inquest was announced in November 2004. Its conclusion was that Ronald Maddison had been the victim of unlawful killing after deliberate exposure to the deadly Sarin nerve gas. Lord Chief Justice Woolf described it as a death at the hands of the State.

Today we know the truth. This opens up the opportunity for some 600 other victims to consider claims for compensation for their suffering. But what else are we not allowed to know? Why are there still documents related to the case that, even after 50 years, are so sensitive that we are not allowed to see them? Much of the work carried out at Porton Down still remains a secret.

THE MURDER OF
STEPHEN RODWAY

---◈---

Purton sits midway between Wootton Bassett and Cricklade, on the brow of a hill with the main road running along its ridge. It curves in the village as it takes its course downhill towards Purton Stoke, once famous for its spa with mineral water bubbling up from a hole in a field. For hundreds of years, the poor of the area visited the 'Salt Hole' for their medicinal fix. It was along this road in 1819 that a brutal murder took place, a murder which had three principal characters: the unfortunate victim, the killer and the lucky-to-escape intended target.

It was early May in 1819. Joseph Pitt was the MP for Cricklade and had recently been elected. These were the days when there were few people who qualified to vote, usually just landowners and wealthy business people only, perhaps two or three hundred to a constituency. Despite their wealth, there was an expectation that their vote would attract a payment. No one viewed this practice as illegal, or immoral. It had gone on for generations. If you were entitled to vote, you expected to be paid to do so. It was still your choice as to who you took the payment from and voted for. Hence, after an election, there were accounts to be settled. It was widely known that Joseph Pitt's agent would be travelling to Cricklade to make the necessary payments and it didn't take a genius to calculate that he would be carrying several hundred pounds. He was an obvious target but, as it happens, he completed his day's work unhindered and returned home unscathed.

We turn to the victim. Stephen Rodway was a coal and salt merchant who lived a contented life in the village of Cricklade with his wife Mary. His son-in-law, a man named Habgood, more or less ran the business for him. On 7 May Habgood bid his father-in-law goodbye as he watched him set off on his black horse heading towards Wootton Bassett. It was about one o'clock in the afternoon and Rodway rode off with a light coloured greatcoat tied up on the saddle before him. A few days before, Habgood had given his father-in-law a Bank of England £5 note, two £1 notes and several other notes all of which he had marked for identification purposes. The value of such notes being so high, he had also recorded their numbers. When Rodway set off towards Wootton Bassett, he was carrying these notes plus a jewelled silver hunting watch and a red leather-covered pocket book.

Rodway completed his day's visit to Wootton Bassett and in the evening was making his way home. At about 9.30 there was the sound of a gunshot, heard by most of the nearby village of Purton Stoke, and Rodway lay dead in the road, with a wound to his chest and robbed of everything valuable on his person. Shortly after, a man was seen riding through the nearby villages on a dark horse which matched the one previously being ridden by Rodway. The description fitted that of a man called Robert Watkins. But more of him later.

Phoebe Greemes lived at Purton Stoke. It was about a quarter past ten and she was riding her horse towards her home when it suddenly shied and she realised that there in the bend of the road was the body of a man, lying on his back, apparently dead. Phoebe made haste towards Stoke where she found Mr Pathe, the solicitor. He returned to the scene with Phoebe, taking with him a man named Packer, and a couple of others followed. There they found the body and examined the man's pockets to see if there was anything which would identify him. All they could find were some bits of small change in his waistcoat pocket.

The body was taken to the Bell Inn at Stoke where Mr Wells, the surgeon from Cricklade, examined it and found it to be still warm and with a single gunshot wound to the chest. Two days later, when the surgeon examined the body in greater detail, he discovered that there was one large wound and two smaller ones about an inch either side. From inside the body was recovered a bullet and the heads of three horseshoe nails; one had lodged in a rib, another in the spine and the third in the lungs. The bullet had severed a main artery which caused almost instant death. There were no other marks on the body to indicate a struggle, nor was there any dirt on his hands. The conclusion drawn was that Rodway had been leaning forward when he was shot and that the bullet and nail heads were all part of the same single shot.

A description of the man seen riding away from the scene of the crime was issued and suspicion soon fell on 25-year-old Robert Watkins. He was tracked down at his Wootton Bassett home where he lived with his father and 16-year-old brother Edward. The premises were searched and although nothing incriminating was found, three bank notes were later traced, all of which were identified as those given to Rodway by his son-in-law and all of which had recently been in Watkins's possession. The pocket book, hunting watch and the remainder of the money were not found and a advertisement was put into the newspapers offering a £10 reward for information as to their whereabouts. It was later discovered that his brother Edward had apparently buried the pistol used in the crime. The brothers were arrested to await their trial, Robert Watkins for murder, Edward as an accessory after the fact.

At the trial no evidence was brought against Edward and

he was released. The prosecution focused its full efforts on Robert Watkins. A local mason, Henry Cox, described how he had seen Watkins at about eight o'clock in the evening in the White Hart Inn at Cricklade on the day of the murder. Watkins, who had with him a large coat, had said that he was suffering from foot problems and would not walk home that night but spend it in the town. William Hicks, a farm labourer, described how, at about half past nine, he was driving sheep at the top of Purton Hill, with a boy called Thomas Eagles. He had passed a man just a few yards away. The man declined to reply when he bade him a good evening and kept his face concealed with his hat down over his eyes and collar erect. He wore a large coat, fitting the description of that seen by Henry Cox, beneath which he appeared to be concealing something, perhaps the pistol.

Ann Seymour described how, some ten minutes after she heard the shot, a man with a coat fitting the same description had passed the cottage where she stood in the doorway, but this man was riding a dark horse and was not walking.

Sophia Cousens testified that she knew Watkins and that he had sent her a letter containing a bank note, with a request that she look after it until he had need of it. Edward Belcher, a draper, gave evidence that Watkins had spent two £1 notes at his premises and produced the notes. They were among those that Habgood had given to his father-in-law, as was that which had been sent to Sophia Cousens. Mr R. Hunt stated he had seen a pistol on a table in Watkins's home a few days before the crime, despite Watkins' denial of having touched a gun in the previous four years.

The evidence was piling up against Watkins but he had one last defence to try. When he was arrested, he had stated that on the evening of the murder he could remember seeing a man fitting the description of the murder victim riding by on a dark horse. A couple of minutes later, he saw another man riding in the same direction, not far behind the victim.

Unknown to Watkins, the man he had tried to implicate had a rock solid alibi, being out of the county at the time. It all added to his apparent guilt.

Throughout the trial, Watkins denied the charge. The judge began his summing up, explaining to the jury that the evidence was overwhelmingly indicating the prisoner's guilt. The pistol had been uncovered and the bank notes traced back to him. It took less than a minute for the jury to declare that Robert Watkins was guilty of murder.

On Friday, 30 July 1819, Robert Watkins made the journey from Fisherton Gaol to Purton Stoke and a place called Moore Stones, now known as Watkins Corner. The convention in those days was for the criminal to be executed as close as practical to the scene of the crime. As he approached the chosen location, the gallows came into view and there before him had gathered one of the largest audiences ever for a public execution. Somewhere between ten and fifteen thousand people had come to witness the spectacle and perhaps to hear his final words. With him were his solicitor Mr Butt, his gaoler Mr Dowding and the Reverend Mr Harrison, prison chaplain. In addition, 200 special constables had been sworn in to ensure the best of order.

Approaching his death, he remained defiantly resolute. The crowd was solemn with not a murmur to muffle the words which Watkins spoke with clarity and confidence. He declared his innocence to the gathered crowd and declined the offer from the chaplain to unburden his soul of all his sins. He stepped to the scaffold with dignity and confidence, taking a prolonged look at his mother as he passed her, nodding her a silent farewell and then shaking hands with her, with no loss of composure.

At the scaffold he prayed in earnest and, at his own request, read aloud Psalm 108, 'Oh God, my heart is ready'. He turned to the crowd and declared 'God bless you all' as the hangman adjusted the rope. It was 2.15 in the afternoon when, still uttering prayers, he dropped to meet his Maker. At that very moment, a huge thunderclap filled the air and the storm continued for a full half hour. Slowly the crowd returned to their homes and in due course of time the body was removed and delivered to Mr Wells, the surgeon, for dissection.

The victim of this crime, Stephen Rodway, was buried on 11 May 1819 in St Mary's churchyard where his grave can still be found today, clearly marked with a large headstone. Thirty one years later his wife Mary joined him in the same plot, having lived to the age of 89.

THE EDINGTON ENIGMA

———————⚙———————

Although King Alfred, also known as Alfred the Great, is most famous for burning the cakes, perhaps he should be better remembered for his successes rather than his failures.

In the overall scheme of things, burning half a dozen cakes pales into insignificance compared to crushing the Danes at the Battle of Edington and saving the kingdom of Wessex from the rampages of the Viking hordes. And proudly the people of Wiltshire have claimed that particular battle honour as their own, fought with men of Wiltshire on Wiltshire soil, at Edington near Westbury. But from over the border in Somerset, there comes a challenge from artist and historian Michael Stirling. He claims, and with reasonable argument, that it is Somerset which deserves the reflected glory and not Wiltshire, for in Somerset there is an Edington and there is strong evidence to suggest that it was there that the battle was fought. Which is correct? That is the mystery.

Alfred came to the throne in AD 871, aged just 21. He was already experienced in battle, having fought the Danes on numerous occasions. During the preceding years, the Danes had slowly taken control of the north and east of England and under their leader Guthrum were pushing into the Wessex of King Alfred. They successfully launched a winter attack on his palace at Chippenham. Alfred fled into the depths of Somerset, hiding in the marshlands with a party of loyal followers at a place called Athelney. This was in the heart of the territory in which he spent his childhood

King Alfred (Courtesy of Michael Stirling, MIDiagE, MSAII)

and where he learnt to hunt, becoming totally familiar with the landscape. It was an area in which he could move freely, undetected by the Danes.

Athelney stood as an isolated island in the middle of the marshes and there Alfred built a fortress. This huge area of marsh was surrounded on three sides by steep sided hills, the Quantocks, the Blackdowns and the Poldens. On the fourth side was the sea. All the Danes could do was to hold the high ground over the Somerset Levels. From high on the Polden

Hills, they dug in and kept watch over the marshlands below, waiting for Alfred's next move. From his fortress, Alfred carried out guerrilla raids on the Danes, a permanent thorn in their side. The Danes had to stay in the area, blocking any opportunity for Alfred to gather forces and become a more serious threat elsewhere. Their need to maintain vigil was constant with Alfred attacking each time a weakness was shown.

Spring came and Alfred had to act. The marshlands would start to dry out and Athelney would be less well defended. He needed a permanent solution and Guthrum had to be pushed back. In May 878, he sent out a message to all the Saxon communities in the west to join the army he would pull together to defeat the Danish hordes. His instructions were to meet at Egbert's Stone and there his forces gathered, men from Somerset, Hampshire and Wiltshire. From there, they marched to Ethandun, the modern translation of which is Edington, and the battle took place. It was hard fought and lasted all day. Alfred's tactics were similar to those used by the Romans, keeping his men close together and interlocking their shields, thrusting their spears through narrow openings. The Danes were on the edge of defeat and fell into retreat. They made their way back to Chippenham where they had wintered. But Alfred's men were resolute and hot on their heels. They besieged the camp at Chippenham and in two weeks the Danes were starved into submission. That at least is the historians' version.

Despite the afterglow of victory, Alfred showed sufficient wisdom to realise that he could not rid the whole country of the Danes, but he could defend Wessex. And so he negotiated a peace treaty with Guthrum which was signed at the village of Wedmore. Guthrum agreed to withdraw all his men from Wessex and, in addition, he and his captains were baptised into Christianity. Alfred then organised Wessex with fortified towns, boroughs, and introduced a system of conscription into the army on a rotational basis. Relative peace came to the West Country. Landowners and serfs could go about their daily business unafraid of attack from the Danes. Alfred extended this success across the Anglo-Saxon world and unified England as we know it today. He deserved the title of 'the Great'.

But let's return to the Edington enigma. Whilst Wiltshire claims the site of Alfred's decisive battle, logic may lead us to believe the glory belongs on the other side of the border. Put yourself in Guthrum's position. Alfred, despite his recent routing at Chippenham, had experienced a number of successes against the Danes. He was a serious threat. Guthrum needed to ensure Alfred was safely contained and not running loose to organize a counter-attack. The logical place for Guthrum and his troops to be was on the southern edge of the Polden Hills, where he could keep watch over the marshlands where he knew Alfred to be. Take a look at the map on the next page and see how Athelney lies beneath the Polden Hills, beneath Somerset's Edington.

Guthrum was not the only Dane with an army in the area. Another called Hubba was planning to join Guthrum and between them sweep the Saxons from the West Country. They needed to combine forces and defeat Alfred. Hubba's boats arrived at the village of Combwich, just across the river at the westerly end of the Polden Hills, but a reception party was waiting for them and they were defeated. Guthrum was unaware of this but I suspect Alfred had received the news.

Alfred knew it was time to attack the Danes on the Polden Ridge. He sent out messengers calling on his forces from across the three counties to gather together to rid their kingdom of the Danes. They responded to the call and, probably under cover of darkness, made their way westward along the Polden Ridge. As day broke, the Danes were taken by surprise as Alfred's men, first those on foot and then those on horse, tore into them.

This raises more questions. Why would Alfred apparently call for his forces to gather at Egbert's Stone near Penselwood? Admittedly it was a central point for those men from the three counties, mostly Somerset and Wiltshire. However, if the battle was to be fought at Edington in Wiltshire, the Wiltshire men would have to go to Penselwood only to travel back again. Likewise, if the battle was fought in Somerset, the Somerset men would have to travel to Penselwood only to make the same journey back. It makes no sense. What would make sense is if they gathered perhaps at the eastern end of the Polden Ridge or even at Alfred's fortress at Athelney?

The other burning question is why would Guthrum

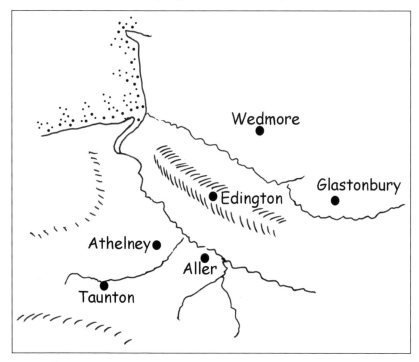

Map showing the location of Somerset's Edington

retreat to Chippenham, when only months before his own forces had stripped it bare of any provisions and he certainly would not receive a warm welcome from the inhabitants? And then he apparently travelled nearly all the way back to Somerset in order to sign the Treaty of Wedmore, just a few miles from the Polden village of Edington. Far more likely is that the treaty was signed shortly after the battle. We also know that Guthrum was baptized into the Christian faith at Aller, near Athelney and Langport.

But where does that leave Wiltshire's claim to the battle honours? The only evidence we have that the Edington where the battle took place is in Wiltshire comes from the contemporary biographer Asser. He recorded the events in considerable detail. In recent times, historians have raised questions over the accuracy of his records but still they claim Wiltshire as the rightful claimant to the honour. They stick with the Wiltshire theory, and I am sure most Wiltshire people will, but from across the border comes a well-reasoned challenge that leaves us with a mystery.

THE MURDEROUS
LORD STOURTON

---❁---

Possibly the most malicious murders ever to take place in
Wiltshire were those of William Hartgill and his wife at
the hands of an evil baron. It was not just the violence of the
final deed that made it so horrific but the way the couple
were hounded and terrorized unmercilessly by an apparent
noble peer of the realm.

When the young Edward VI was on the throne, William,
Lord Stourton, was charged with the responsibility of
safeguarding one of the king's palaces in Boulogne. He had
been a loyal and trusted friend to the royal family. Born in
Stourton around 1484, he married Elizabeth Dudley in his
early thirties and their union was blessed in 1521 with a son,
Charles, destined one day to inherit his father's title. On
16 September 1548, William, Lord Stourton died whilst still
serving the king's interests in Boulogne. His wife, Dame
Elizabeth, and their son received the news. Dame Elizabeth
went into mourning and travelled to stay with her old
friends the Hartgills who lived a few miles away at
Kilmington.

Charles meanwhile inherited his title and became the 8th
Baron Stourton. But Charles was greedy and malicious and
wanted more than just the title. He wanted everything that
his father owned, including his money and lands. The
problem was that the widow Dame Elizabeth, Charles's
mother, was still alive and it was she who held the purse

strings. It was not an arrangement which suited the young, arrogant and ambitious Charles. He had power; he had money; he wanted more. He wanted his mother to release the financial reins, hand over a large sum of money and give him a guarantee that she would never again marry, an action which would put any residual inheritance at risk.

There was clearly an absence of the normal loving relationship between mother and son. Here was a man determined not to lose his inheritance and, if at all possible, acquire it prematurely. He was an evil baron of the worst kind who cared not a jot for his mother's welfare, only the inheritance and power to which she acted as a barrier. As the years passed, so his patience expired and he was driven to desperate measures.

Unable to persuade his mother to concede, he decided to put pressure on her closest friends, William Hartgill and his wife. This wasn't gentle persuasion, but threats against person and property. William Hartgill, however, remained a trusted and loyal friend to Dame Elizabeth and gave her good counsel. He advised her that she should only hand over control of her finances and property if there was a guarantee from her son of an annual income to provide for her.

Charles Stourton was outraged and a bitter feud erupted between himself and William Hartgill. It was on a Whit Sunday morning that events took a most unpleasant turn. Charles Stourton took several men with him on a visit to Kilmington church where he knew he would find Hartgill. His men were armed with bows and with guns. The villagers watched his approach and feared trouble from the baron's group. John Hartgill, William's son, was at the church and was warned of their coming. Leaving the church he drew his sword and ran to his father's house as fast as he was able, making it just in time as Charles's bowmen unleashed a volley of arrows which fortunately landed harmlessly all around him.

The Hartgills' house adjoined the church and this offered a convenient sanctuary as the couple with their son and a handful of servants ascended the bell tower. Young John had managed to grab a cross-bow, a long bow, a supply of arrows and a gun. From the house he opened fire on Charles's men who were in the open and he managed to repel them, all except for about ten men who had already invaded the church. One of those he had wounded in the shoulder. John knew that as long as his parents remained in the tower they would be relatively safe and so, encouraged by his father, he rode to the king's court to report the baron's evil behaviour.

Back at Kilmington, realising the son had ridden off, Charles returned to the church with his men and continued their assault on the besieged occupants, a siege which continued for three days. John Hartgill meanwhile, on the Monday evening, had informed the king of events at home and Edward sent orders for Sir Thomas Speak to go to the rescue of the Hartgills and to take Charles captive and deliver him to the court. Speak arrived on the Wednesday, released the Hartgills and arrested Charles. The king committed him to the Fleet prison but before long he was released.

Now even angrier, he again sought revenge. One of his men stole William Hartgill's best horse and took it to Stourton Park. There they shot it with a cross-bow, claiming that Hartgill had been hunting on Stourton land. They stole Hartgill's cattle and burned his crops. They did everything they could to ruin him.

King Edward died and Queen Mary took the throne. Conveniently she was just across the border in Hampshire and William Hartgill took the opportunity to petition her to command Charles to cease his vengeful acts. The Queen commanded both men to attend her and there, with her council, she listened to the case. Hartgill won the day and

Queen Mary commanded Charles to promise to compensate Hartgill for the damage he had caused. Charles conceded and agreed that if Hartgill and his son John would visit him at Stourton, they would be granted not only Charles's good will but full restoration for their lost and destroyed cattle and crops. A member of the court went with them to ensure the pledge was fulfilled.

The group set off from the queen's court and rode towards Stourton, Charles in the lead, William Hartgill and the queen's representative towards the rear, followed by Hartgill's son John. As they rode along a lane approaching Stourton, a band of Charles's men rode out from the woods and ambushed the young man riding at the rear. Before John Hartgill could draw his sword, four wounds had already been inflicted on him. He fell from his horse and was left for dead. Half an hour later, he recovered sufficiently to regain his horse and ride to the safety of Richard Mumpesson who lived at nearby Maiden Bradley.

When news of this latest attack on the Hartgills reached Queen Mary, Charles was summoned to appear before the Star Chamber, an all powerful court under the control of the Crown. Charles was fined and imprisoned again in the Fleet gaol. Somehow he managed to manipulate his release and returned to Stourton where he was showing no signs of penitence. Indeed matters were to escalate to a higher and more disastrous level.

On arriving at his home, he sent a message to the Hartgills that he was ready to make amends and invited them to visit him at Stourton Caundle. The Hartgills justifiably did not feel safe meeting him on his own ground but agreed to meet him at Kilmington church. The Hartgills arrived first and waited within the church. When Charles arrived, he had a party of 60 or so of his people with him. He immediately went to the church house adjoining the church and sent word that the Hartgills should join him there. Suspicious of his motives, they refused to meet him anywhere other than in the church, where they knew he dare not harm them, or in the open, where others could witness any misdeeds he instigated. It was agreed that they should meet at a table on the open green by the church.

The two parties stepped forward towards the table, the Hartgills taking some comfort that at last they would receive compensation as they watched Charles place a purse upon the table. Charles declared that he had been ordered to recompense them and the money was there to be collected. As they approached the table, his tone changed from reconciliation to anger. His message altered likewise as he declared that he was arresting them for felony. A dozen or so of his men stepped forward and took the Hartgills prisoner. Their hands were bound behind their backs. Young John Hartgill was also punched severely around the head as he too was bound. Hearing the disturbance, John's wife appeared at the front door of a nearby house, only to be struck with a sword to the head, leaving her close to death as she collapsed to the ground.

William Hartgill and his wife were then taken to the parson's house at Kilmington where they were left, still bound. About an hour after midnight they were moved again, this time to Bonham, a house near Stourton where they were confined in separate rooms, thrown on the floor with no food nor drink and with nothing to lie on. After two hours they were on the move again. This time, in the open and under cover of darkness, they were clubbed apparently to death. Four of Charles's men were responsible for the killing of the couple. The bodies were taken to a passageway into his house with Charles leading the way with a lighted candle. But the Hartgills were not dead and William in particular began to groan. Charles was concerned that a French priest who was staying there at the time would hear them and so this minor irritation was resolved by slitting the couple's throats before throwing their bodies into a dungeon where two of Charles's men dug a pit in which they were buried.

Word soon leaked out as to the dastardly deed perpetrated by Lord Stourton. Sir Anthony Hungerford, investigating the crime, had the bodies dug up and found them to have been buried wearing the same clothes which they were wearing on the last occasion they were seen at the green next to the church. They had been covered with earth, then two layers of paving stones and all of that covered with a mass of wood shavings.

Charles and his four henchmen were taken for trial. Apart from the murder of William Hartgill and his wife, other crimes were revealed. Three of his servants had set fire to a barn owned by Thomas Chaffin, one of his tenants. Charles had then accused Chaffin of allowing the barn to burn without his consent or knowledge as his landlord and thereby swindled the man out of twelve hundred sheep and all of his oxen and horses by way of recompense. From other tenants he had taken cattle and other animals.

Charles's guilt was soon established. In March 1556, he and his four henchmen were taken from the Tower of London to Salisbury, with overnight stops at Hounslow and Staines on the way. The custom of the country was that barons should not suffer the same death as lesser mortals. They were entitled to execution by beheading. The evil deeds of the 8th Baron of Stourton were such that he was denied that privilege and was sentenced to death by hanging as a common criminal.

On 6 March, the evil baron was hanged in the market place at Salisbury where gallows had been erected awaiting his arrival. His four henchmen were taken to the scene of their crime and hanged there.

After his death, Stourton's friends asked the bishop to consent to his burial in Salisbury Cathedral. The bishop refused on the grounds of the baron's lack of worthiness but was torn between that and the convention that such nobility were buried within the cathedral. He relented but only when Stourton's friends agreed to the condition that the silken halter used to hang Stourton should be suspended over his grave to indicate his villainy.

BEATING THE RETREAT

---◉---

William Drury had fought for the Parliamentarian cause during the English Civil War as a member of Cromwell's Model Army. He had served proudly as soldier and drummer boy but, after his demobilisation, had fallen on hard times. Now just an old soldier, he took on the life of a vagrant and beggar. He had developed a technique for acquiring money which was almost unique at the time. Today we have our modern day street buskers, many of them highly talented, who add colour to an otherwise dull day. Others, perhaps less talented, move on when the rewards are minimal. But when someone is really bad, they have to go. William Drury's technique was to be such an intolerable nuisance that the locals would pay him not to play. In March 1662 he had chosen the village of Ludgershall to benefit from his entertainment and for a while he was partially successful. The problem was that Ludgershall was so small that it didn't matter where he moved to, you could still hear him, irritatingly beating out his drum tattoo, beating the retreat, wherever you were in the village. He was also using apparently forged notes for his purchases.

The drumming was incessant. The residents were close to despair when John Mompesson stepped in. He was a magistrate from the neighbouring village of South Tidworth where he lived at Tedworth House. Driven mad by the continuous drumming, he ordered the bailiff to arrest Drury as a vagrant and to bring Drury before him. Drury produced papers to show that he was not a vagrant, that he had rights to be in the parish, but the magistrate declared them to be forgeries. Mompesson confiscated the offending item, the drum, and had Drury held in custody pending a report from his former commanding officer.

Drury wasn't in prison for long. He escaped but his drum was still under lock and key. Weeks later, Drury had not been found and the bailiff couldn't decide what should happen to the drum, and so he sent it to Mompesson at his home at Tedworth House. At the time, Mompesson was away in London and his wife took delivery of the drum. She was soon to regret her action. What if the owner returned to get his drum? How could she defend herself and her children against such a villain? Each night, she nervously retired to bed, half expecting a bang on the door or the smashing of a window. And then it happened. There was a loud rapping on the doors around the house and tapping on the windows.

The following day, her husband returned and, in a visibly distressed state, she told him of her fears and experience. That night, there was again loud rapping on the front door. Mompesson grabbed a pair of pistols and opened the door, by which time it was another door that was being rapped on and then another, yet each time with no one to be seen. The disturbed couple retired to bed and then the knocking came from the roof. Quietly at first, but slowly gaining in volume, there came the sound of a tattoo being beaten on a drum, beating the retreat.

Night after night, the visitations continued, sometimes several nights in a row followed by a few nights of calm. Mrs Mompesson was convinced the disturbances were in some way linked to the confiscated drum. In desperation, Mompesson destroyed the offending item. Having done so, the sounds from outside stopped, but from then on they continued even louder from within and always coming from the room where once the drum had been stored.

At this time, Mrs Mompesson was pregnant and went

away for the birth. On her return, peace had been restored to the house and for three weeks life returned to normal. But then the visitations came back with a vengeance. The noises became more frequent, louder and longer lasting. The banging of the drum would go on for hours outside of the children's bedroom doors. The drum was still beating the retreat. Within weeks, scratching sounds could be heard under the children's beds which would lift up and down in the night. For their own safety, the children were moved into the attic but the noises followed them.

Throughout this experience, the family remained resolute, determined not to be driven out by whatever supernatural force was plaguing them. It was as though a battle were going on. Noises turned into activity as the stubborn presence escalated the proceedings by throwing objects around the house. Finally Mr Mompesson conceded and called on the help of the vicar, the Reverend Craig. Kneeling at the base of the children's bed, and praying in earnest, the battle between the forces of good and evil commenced. Furniture, clothes, ornaments, anything big enough and hard enough to hurt was thrown at the vicar by whatever was present in the room. Louder and louder, and more fervently he prayed as each object hit him. It was all to no avail. The disturbances continued. Just who or what was causing the disruption to the household could only be imagined. The drum was clearly a link to the explanation. Could it be a ghost? To the best of the family's knowledge Drury, the last owner of the now destroyed drum, was still alive. Can living persons haunt a house? Could it be the drum itself? It remained a mystery.

The following year, William Drury was in trouble again, this time for stealing. He was locked up in Gloucester gaol and there he boasted to an inmate that he had cursed a house in Wiltshire in revenge for the confiscation of his drum. In the 17th century, such an statement was tantamount to confessing to witchcraft. It was a foolish thing to say. However, boasting was one thing but there was no evidence for a case of witchcraft and so he was simply tried for stealing a pig. Sentenced to transportation, he left these shores never to return. And from that day hence, Tedworth House returned to a peaceful existence.

More than a hundred years later, in an unrelated incident, a story unfolded on Salisbury Plain of another drummer boy. It was June 1786 and two sailors were crossing the Plain bound for Salisbury. Their ship had docked at Plymouth and their pockets had been blessed with the end of voyage pay. The weather on the Plain had taken a nasty turn. Storm clouds had gathered and darkened the sky. They were no doubt pleased to be ashore and not at sea in such weather but then there was a great flash of lightning and a crack of thunder. The previously calm day turned into a torrential downpour with the wind blowing at such force that they could barely stand. One of the sailors, Gervase Matcham, was inexplicably terrified, as if he had seen a ghost. Storms at sea were commonplace, and he had never previously shown such fear of thunder and lightning. But this was something different. He curled into a ball with his arms over his head, lying in the road, quivering and begging for mercy.

John Sheppard, his travelling companion, could not understand what had happened. It was not as though they had actually been struck by the lightning but here was his shipmate apparently going berserk. He tried to calm him and to discover just what was wrong. Matcham said that a woman had appeared before him, only to be replaced by a giant boulder. It was as if there was a mystical force blocking his way. He became convinced that he would not survive the storm unless he confessed to the dreadful deed he had committed many years before. It was as though the storm had become his judge and jury. He allowed his confession to unfold as he related his crime to his companion.

Several years before, he had been travelling with a drummer boy who was carrying a purse of money to his father, a recruiting sergeant. Matcham had suggested to the lad that they could stop at an inn for refreshments. For some reason, the lad's refusal to stop angered Matcham who attacked the young drummer boy. One single blow and he was down with Matcham trying to snatch the money. The boy resisted but Matcham drew a knife and slit his throat.

Matcham escaped, went to London, worked on the river and then became a sailor travelling far and wide, his involvement in the crime having been detected, but his whereabouts remaining unknown until his confession in that storm on Salisbury Plain. The following morning, Matcham confessed to the mayor of Salisbury, who found the whole story very hard to believe. However, he had to treat it as a serious possibility and made enquiries concerning whether or not a drummer boy had been murdered some time before. Thanks to the story then being published in the newspapers, sufficient information came forward to confirm the grim events of all those years before. One source was able to provide a description of the man sought for the murder, which included details of a missing tooth. The description was a perfect fit for Matcham who not long after faced the jury. The outcome and penalty were inevitable.

HAUNTED WILTSHIRE

———————— ✿ ————————

Wiltshire is no stranger to the supernatural. Crop circles, strange lights in the sky, the mysteries of Avebury and Stonehenge, all add to the tapestry of Wiltshire's inexplicable happenings. Nowadays we hear all kinds of explanations, especially from those who follow alternative lifestyles. These fashions come and go, but where ghosts are concerned, there is a comforting consistency with ghostly sightings of today bearing the same hallmark as ghostly sightings of hundreds of years ago. And there is a reassuring cross-section of Wiltshire society involved, from monks and other members of the clergy to the aristocracy.

In 1840, in the village of Allington, the curate and a group of his parishioners were enjoying a most convivial evening. The company and food had been excellent and spirits were high, thanks to the plentiful supply of alcoholic beverages available that evening. Even the curate had partaken of more than was good for him, so much so that when the time came to go home, he struggled to mount his horse. With one foot in the stirrup, he clutched the horn of the saddle, gave a great pull upwards and fell backwards. Second attempt, foot in the stirrup, another giant heave and up he shot with such force that he flew straight over the top and landed head first on the ground on the other side.

His companions, having calmed themselves from the initial uncontrollable laughter, rushed up to see what damage he might have inflicted upon himself only to find that the fall had broken his neck. Panic set in. Such was their own state of inebriation that no one could think what would be the sensible thing to do. Whatever the solution was, they had to act quickly before anyone from outside the group realised what had happened. For some unknown reason, their decision was to throw his body down the well!

From that day hence, horses passing by would shy away and act nervously as long as they were in the well's vicinity. No one had been able to discover why. The group of friends never revealed what happened that evening. To a man, they took their secret to their graves. The truth was only discovered some years later when a lady who had been present at the high-spirited party revealed the truth on her deathbed.

Not far from Allington is Cholderton House at Cholderton. This also appears to be haunted by a clergyman. In common with the curate of Allington, he too disappeared down a well. The cause of his death remains a mystery. What we do know is that in 1896 he vanished and at the head of the well were his slippers, neatly placed on its rim. Did he slip, fall or was he pushed?

Another member of the clergy whose ghostly presence is frequently felt is the hunchbacked monk of Highworth, to the north of Swindon. It is at the King and Queen Inn where the most frequent visitations occur. The inn is believed to be at least 500 years old but its history as part of the former premises of a monastery dates back even earlier. It appears that a monk, a hunchback who was an incumbent at the monastery, had broken his vow of chastity. Another version claims that his crime was stealing a loaf of bread. The latter is most unlikely in that monks were well treated generally and would have had no need to steal bread. Breaking a vow of chastity, however, has a greater ring of credibility. Whatever his crime, his punishment was to be executed and his body was hung in a passageway outside of the inn as we know it today. Ever since, his ghost has haunted the inn and the nearby church. He wanders around in his long white robes with his hood up, mostly concealing his face, albeit those who have seen inside the hood describe it as a dull grey space where his face should be, with darker patches where his absent eyes fail to appear.

There are believed to be old passages which pass from the inn to the nearby church and upstairs is a room once used as a courtroom. Here villains were tried and, where appropriate, sentenced to death. Perhaps it was here that the hunchbacked monk heard his fate. In more recent times his ghostly form has frequently been seen. Some have observed him rising through the floorboards where a passage exists below, presumably walking a route where once there would have been steps up from that passage. Often he has been seen walking towards the old stables. He has caused a table to levitate and sudden changes in temperature are attributed to his presence. Even the dogs have sensed his closeness. One dog simply sat in a corner, growling at the unseen form. On one occasion, a landlord let his dogs loose into the yard believing a burglar to be present only to have the dogs back away, their hackles standing erect. The landlord could see the person through the darkness, yet could not get the dogs to respond. Instead he approached the figure himself, only for it to disappear through a wall.

At the nearby St Michael's church, the monk's ghost has been at the south door in the middle of the day, walking across the altar area and around the outside of the church. On another occasion he walked down the aisle and made his exit through the west door, passing ethereally through heavy curtains as he made his way outside. Frequently he has been seen walking from the church towards the King and Queen Inn, or along the adjacent Sheep Street and across the market place travelling between the church and the site of the old monastery.

We must now go to the peaceful ruins of Wardour Castle

near Tisbury. This was once the scene of a violent siege during the time of the English Civil War and it offers another chance to meet a ghost. The spirit in residence is that of Blanche, Lady Arundel. It was in May 1643 that the castle was attacked by Sir Edward Hungerford, a commander with the Parliamentarian forces. The Arundels were staunch supporters of the royal family and were not going to concede the castle to the Roundheads without putting up the stiffest defence. For five days, the castle and its few dozen occupants came under attack. Lady Arundel herself was actively involved, leading the women of the castle in keeping the fighting men supplied with loaded muskets, food and water. With over a thousand armed troops outside, the valiant defence was bound to end in favour of the besiegers. Despite the inevitable, Lady Arundel managed to negotiate an honourable settlement, one whereby no one from within the castle would be punished. Terms were agreed and the castle surrendered. The defenders were taken prisoner and, after a mock trial, executed, the betrayed Lady Arundel amongst them. Is it any wonder that her ghost now haunts the grounds?

Towards the end of that year, Henry Arundel led an attempt to regain the castle. No one knows if the climactic end was planned or unplanned, but somehow a powder store held in a tunnel beneath the castle was ignited and blew up the castle. The remains were left to fall into ruin. They now form a enchanting backdrop to the landscaped grounds where the spirit of Lady Arundel still walks as she drifts along the lakeside taking her evening stroll.

Perhaps Wiltshire's most celebrated ghost is that of the Duke of Buckingham who apparently shops at Debenhams in Salisbury! It was in 1485 that King Richard III formed the opinion that he had been betrayed by the Duke of Buckingham having received intelligence that the Duke was raising arms against him. Buckingham had helped to place

Richard III on the throne, perhaps using the opportunity as a stepping stone to his own elevation. But Buckingham was also in league with Henry Tudor. Inevitably, Buckingham was apprehended and taken to Salisbury where the king was already present with his large army. The outcome was predictable and on 16 December, Buckingham was beheaded in the market place, immediately outside the Blue Boar and Saracen's Head taverns. Legend has it that on the anniversary of the Duke's death, he walks slowly out into the yard only to vanish again, perhaps replaying the occasion of his execution.

Today a blue plaque, on the side of the Debenhams department store, marks the spot where the execution took place. Within the store can now be found the Blue Boar restaurant which is believed to be on the spot where the Duke spent his last night. It is his ghost which now walks the store at night, mostly restricting his movements to the top floor. One has to feel sorry for the telecommunications engineer who was once working in the attic and left in terror having been clasped on the shoulder by an unseen cold hand. For an engineer to leave his tool box behind, there has to be a genuine reason.

In parts of the store, cobblestones from the days of the duke can still be found. Attempts to move them have only resulted in the most unusual occurrences. In 1839, a skeleton was discovered beneath them, minus its head and one of its arms, each of these items almost certainly having been taken to London for public display in the wake of an execution! Could this have been the remains of the Duke?

AN ANCIENT AND
MODERN MYSTERY

———————— ✿ ————————

Crop circles: natural phenomenon or major hoax? Across the world the question has raged on and will continue to provoke speculation for years to come. Of one thing we can be certain, Wiltshire is the crop circle centre of the world. But what are they and what is their cause?

Crop circles are patterns typically formed in fields of cereal crops: wheat, rye, oats, barley, oilseed rape, any crop which grows thin and tall, where the stem of the plant is prone to bending. Viewed from the air, the crop circle appears as an area of the crop which has been bent over in a circular direction, as if the crop has been almost flattened by a mini tornado. Imagine two people with a long length of rope. One person stands absolutely still while the other person, keeping the rope at full stretch walks in a circle around the first person, until the circle is complete. Imagine that planks are attached along the entire length of the rope. As the circle is formed, the planks flatten the area they cover, beating down the crop over which they pass. Some stems will bend and bounce back, others will snap and stay down – and there you have a crop circle. But it's not a true crop circle, not one which occurred naturally. It is at best a demonstration, at worst a hoax.

The difference with genuine crop circles is that the stems of the plants are bent but not snapped, as if they have been gently coaxed over into that position and their cell structure prefers them to stay that way – for the time being. Within such circles there are no signs of anyone treading in the area, no snapping stems here and there from the 'artists' as they went about their work. Already we find ourselves entering the world of the two camps of those who study crop circles, the believers and the sceptics. The truth undoubtedly lies somewhere between the two but there is a third camp of interested parties who do nothing to help either the sceptics or the believers to reach the truth, and they are the hoaxers.

Let's focus on the naturally occurring circles. I recently spent some time on the Serengeti Plains in Tanzania, dry and dusty, visibility extending miles across the flatlands where little vegetation exists to obscure the view. Occasionally the monotony of the landscape is broken by the ridge of a hill. During the hours of daylight, mini whirlwinds or tornadoes appear from nowhere along the lower side of these ridges, made clearly visible by the plumes of dust lifting skyward within their vortex, known as 'dust devils' to the local Masai. They disappear as rapidly as they arise and in their wake, circular patterns are left on the ground.

We have all visited the coast on occasions and there, along the windswept shores, we have seen trees and shrubs shaped by the prevailing winds. They appear to lean inwards, towards the land, naturally shaped on the landward side, but with a long, gentle and straight slope on the windward side. Nature has shaped these trees. It is not man's hand, no pruning or snapping of branches, just stems firmly fixed by nature in their gently bending positions, their plant cells having shaped them that way. Genuine crop circles are similar in that the plant stems are bent but not broken. In time they will straighten up and no one will know the difference.

Crop circles are not a new phenomenon. They appeared at least as far back as the superstitious times of the 17th century, the days when witches were being purged from our society. A crop circle discovered in a field of oats was explained away as having been created by the 'mowing devils', the fairies or pixies, and they always appeared overnight. If you were the peasant responsible for the care of the field concerned, it was the easiest way to account for the damage on your patch, by placing the blame elsewhere. Naturally if someone in the community was suspected of being a witch, such a circle would be sufficient evidence to permit a conviction.

Crops circles continued to be reported through the 18th and 19th centuries and on into the 20th, but it was in the late 1970s that crop circle mania began and it really took off in the 1980s. In 1978 a pattern of five crop circles in the form of a Celtic cross were formed near Warminster. Conveniently for those who seek alternative solutions, these came in the wake of the reported sightings of a number of UFOs. There rapidly followed a dramatic increase in the number of crop circles being identified. From the ten or eleven perhaps per year, there were suddenly over 150 in a season. In 1988 they were appearing at the rate of ten a week. One has to be suspicious of the dramatic increase in occurrences.

Conveniently for the media, crop circles come in the summer months when other news is at a premium. The publicity the circles receive appears to trigger a rash of fresh crop circles in their wake. Statistically it is not a case of the more crop circles there are, the more publicity, but the other way around. The publicity brings out the hoaxers and of that there is no doubt. As the publicity fades away, so the crop circles need to become even more elaborate in order to maintain the required level of attention. Instead of the occasional single circular crop depressions, patterns of multiple circles appear, forming Celtic cross shapes, spirals and advanced geometric patterns. Rapidly they become less and less credible as a natural phenomenon but equally of greater interest to the media who need 'interesting' pictures in preference to reality. In 1987, one crop carried the message 'WEARENOTALONE', supposedly from some extra-terrestrial being. Now put yourself in the position of an extraterrestrial who wanted the humans on earth to know that you were out there. Wouldn't you declare 'You are not alone' rather than 'We are not alone'?

Further doubt has to be cast over the explosion of crop circles simply from the fact that they are all produced overnight and never in a field which is being watched. Overnight vigils and the use of modern technology such as infra-red photography and remote-controlled cameras have revealed nothing. In 1989, 60 observers maintained an eight-night observation in an exercise labelled Operation Blackbird. Nothing happened in any of the areas being observed other than the overnight creation of a series of ten circles and three straight lines at Bratton near Westbury. The same night lights had appeared in the sky over the area where the crop circles later appeared. Whilst believers immediately broke into an excited frenzy, declaring this was clearly an alien force trying to make contact, annoyingly for those involved in the operation, it proved to be a hoax. If it is nature's hand which shapes these circles, whether it be the wind or the earth's magnetism, surely nature doesn't stop because someone is there to observe. Far more likely is that the hoaxers simply choose a different venue.

In September 1991 two hoaxers, Doug Bower and Dave Chorley, confessed to the creation of numerous crop circles. It was a year in which over 200 crop circles were reported. Doug and Dave even demonstrated on television how ropes and planks were used to create the effect. However, we have to question whether or not two men could create 200 circles across the county in a limited number of days. Such a volume of complex circles was way beyond the capabilities of two men working on their own in the dark. In 2000,

Bishops Cannings resident Matthew Williams confessed to the creation of crop circles and was fined £140 including costs for damage to a field at West Overton. There are clearly many more hoaxers out there.

So why should people create these hoaxes? In the main it must be the same mentality that causes people to generate computer viruses, an inner urge to be destructive, or creative, and yet remain undetected. Commercial gain could also be an influence. At least one Wiltshire farmer was able to turn the circles to his financial benefit, charging for admission to the field and selling 'crop circle' mugs and T-shirts. But not all of these crop circles are hoaxes.

There have been nights when numerous crop circles have appeared across the county. It would take quite an organisation to produce all of these simultaneously and undetected. Some of those crop formations were of a complicated nature and are surely the work of hoaxers. Their complex nature naturally draws the attention of the media. But there are simple formations which go almost unnoticed. In amongst these, there will almost certainly be genuine, naturally formed crop circles. A US-based team of biophysicists has analysed the stems of plants from circles believed to be naturally created. The cellular structure of such stems has been proven to be incompatible with that which is caused by man-made flattening of the crop. Indeed they claim it to be more akin to the effect caused by electrical or magnetic forces such as are present in thunderstorms or where there is a large build-up of static electricity.

So let's take a summary look at the evidence. We have records of crop circles dating back hundreds of years, but in relatively small numbers and they are simple in form. In 1983 a labourer witnessed the creation of a circle as he looked down from the Ridgeway near Lavington. From about 400 yards away, he saw a spinning cloud of dust, just like the 'dancing devils' I have observed in the Serengeti. It appeared and disappeared with no sign of its approach or movement away from the scene. It simply happened on the spot and dissipated leaving a circle in its wake. Now and again witnesses to these formations will refer to a high frequency buzzing sound, or a sense of the presence of static electricity.

Geographically there is a preponderance of circles on the leeward side of hills during calm atmospheric conditions. This could support the theory of the presence of buzzing sounds and static electricity. In dry weather, where light winds have stirred up dust particles, a resulting build-up of static is quite plausible. This would not only account for the buzzing sounds but the occasional references to a dull glow. It all fits in with theories of the natural creation of crop circles from wind and atmospheric conditions. We can also understand why Wiltshire is the prime source for crop circles in that the topography of the landscape lends itself to their formation, not to the exclusion of the rest of the world but simply in preference to most of it. Such theories have much credibility.

Then we have the explosion of occurrences, especially in the 1980s and 1990s when highly complex and increasingly sophisticated patterns were being created. Those patterns were all produced overnight and the 'creator', whether man or nature, demonstrated a particular shyness, refusing to perform under observation. They have varied from the imaginative and sophisticated to the ludicrous, and detract grossly from the serious investigation which the subject merits. They have become increasingly complex as scorn has been poured on them, as if suffering from some severe attention-seeking syndrome. Unless you take aliens seriously, these occurrences of crop circles must be identified as the work of the hoax community or, at best, the work of frustrated artists.

So, in amongst the ridiculous and the artistic, we have

genuine crop circles, simple patterns which have existed across Wiltshire ever since man took to farming, circles created by nature's hand. The real mystery surrounds the identification and justification of those who go out under cover of darkness to create the remainder.

BIZARRE MURDERS

———————————————❂———————————————

Historically speaking, the punishment for murder has been the death penalty until quite recent times. There have however always been circumstances in which it has been impossible to apply such a sentence.

For example, no one has ever been executed for self murder, as suicide was regarded as in years gone by! In 1773, Richard Francis was the mayor and coroner for Marlborough. In that role he oversaw the inquest into the death of Thomas Tarrant, a local barber who *'did feloniously voluntarily and of his malice aforethought kill, poison and murder himself. Thomas Tarrant not having the fear of God before his Eyes but being seduced and moved by the instigation of the Devil at Marlborough at a certain publick house known as "At the Lamb" being then and there alone on Saturday the 4 September did voluntarily and feloniously with a potion of Arsenick or some other poisonous drug poison himself. The deceased at the time of his death had not any Lands or Tenements Goods or Chattles except his wearing apparell.'*

Poor Thomas Tarrant must have been in a truly depressed state to commit suicide, and then is found guilty of self-murder. The mayor almost makes it sound as if he had killed himself three times – 'kill, poison and murder himself'. Punishing someone for self-murder is clearly quite difficult and so the best that Richard Francis could do was to order that the deceased be buried 'in the King's highway near the common at the said borough and town'. The burial of villains on the highway was common practice, especially so at crossroads.

Another unusual aspect of unexpected deaths until Victorian times was the claiming of a 'deodand', which was defined as a personal belonging which had caused the death of a person, and for that reason was given to God. In other words, whatever caused the unexpected death was forfeited to the Crown and then originally used for pious purposes. So if a cart ran over a man and killed him, it was forfeited as a deodand. Thus the authorities would lay claim to the horse and cart, probably sell it and then use the proceeds to feed the poor. In one example, after a heavy night's drinking, two men got into a brawl. One punched the other so hard that the victim fell back and his head hit a door knocker which cracked his skull. He died from the wound. The human murderer was never caught but the innocent owner of the door, who was quietly tucked up in bed at the time of the incident, had to forfeit the door knocker.

Fifteen-year-old John Pitthouse lived with his parents, Robert and Mary Pitthouse, in Ogbourne St Andrew. In July 1774, he was riding a horse which belonged to his uncle, William Pitthouse, the local blacksmith. On the day concerned, John was riding through Marlborough when the horse shied. Thomas Peck and John Dance, who later gave evidence of the incident, watched as they saw the horse rear up and throw its rider. Poor John Pitthouse's foot was stuck in the stirrup and as the horse galloped off in the direction of St Peter's churchyard, John hit the ground and was dragged all the way to the church, his head bouncing unmercifully along the rough and stony road.

By the time the horse came to a standstill, John Pitthouse was dead. The local surgeon, Mr Henry Hope, examined the body and found the cause of death to be a fractured skull. The records of the inquest not only reported the cause of death but also the combined value of the horse and saddle at

£1. The combined value was clearly significant in that both horse and saddle were equally to blame, one for failing to stop and the other for failing to release the rider. The deodand was therefore set at £1. One can only assume the fee was collected from the blacksmith, who was the owner of both items.

Perhaps the most bizarre murder, if indeed it was a murder, was that of the young child William Bayntun, apparently by witchcraft. The story begins with the lad's grandfather, Sir Edward Bayntun, a man who owned vast estates and who was the head of a most powerful family, a family in which power was seen to corrupt. Sir Edward married Elizabeth Sulliard and from that marriage came two sons, Andrew followed by Edward junior. Elizabeth died, Sir Edward remarried and a stepbrother Henry was born to join Andrew and Edward junior. When Sir Edward died, his titles and the greater part of his estates passed to his eldest son Andrew. This included Bromham, between Chippenham and Devizes. A lesser but adequate property called The Ivy at Rowden went to the second son Edward. By this time, Henry the stepbrother was still just twelve years old and living with his mother.

In 1564, Andrew, by now Sir Andrew, died leaving a daughter Anne who was looked after in her father's will but the greater part of the estate, and the title which went with it, was inherited by Andrew's younger brother, who now became Sir Edward. Edward had meanwhile married Agnes Rhys and a son William had been born shortly before his uncle Andrew's death. The baby William became heir apparent to a huge estate and fortune. William was born when his father was 47 years old. Life expectancy in the 16th century was not particularly long and so Edward's younger step-brother Henry could potentially have inherited the family fortune if Edward had conveniently died with no son to inherit the estate – but he now had one. Henry on the other hand already had three sons, virtually nothing to leave them, and two daughters. He was no doubt envious of his step-brother's wealth.

Sadly, the young William died as an infant and Henry's hopes for the possible inheritance increased dramatically. In all probability it was a natural infant mortality, but these were superstitious times and there was an undoubted Cain and Abel relationship between the two half-brothers. Edward suspected his brother Henry, or more probably his wife, of causing the death of the child in order to increase the prospect of the inheritance. If that were the case, then Edward's life was also probably under threat, at least until he produced another male heir. But how could the murder of his infant son have been carried out? Witchcraft became suspected and Edward and Agnes strongly suspected a woman by the name of Agnes Mylles who was reputed to practise witchcraft.

In Somerset at that time there lived a lady called Jane Marsh. She was reputed to have the powers to identify witches. The Justices of the Assizes for the county of Wiltshire had no idea as to how the child had died or who may have caused the death, but they were confident enough in the powers of Jane Marsh to call for her services and had her brought to Salisbury to assist in their enquiries. She was taken to the place of the suspicious death and there, using her unique powers, she determined that Agnes Mylles had caused the death of the child by witchcraft. She continued by declaring that the witch's services had been obtained by the enticement of Dorothy Bayntun, the wife of Edward's half-brother, Henry.

Agnes Mylles was duly taken to Fisherton where she was hanged for witchcraft. With hindsight this may have seemed a little hasty in that the principal witness later proved somewhat unreliable. But Sir Edward Bayntun was a powerful man and no doubt he ensured that not only was his half-brother disgraced but the accused witch was disposed of with much haste lest any evidence should occur which might contradict his case against her.

Henry and his accused wife Dorothy, as could be expected, defended their position vigorously. Their argument was well reasoned. They claimed that Edward and his wife must have paid Jane Marsh to make the accusations against themselves and Agnes Mylles. It was certainly convenient that she pointed the accusing finger at the very same people that Edward and Agnes Bayntun had suggested as those to blame. Henry, determined to prove his innocence, had Jane Marsh locked up in Sarum prison with the message that there she would rot until she confessed to lying about his or his wife's involvement in the death of their nephew. The only way Jane would ever see the light of day was to confess and so, after six months in the prison cell, that is what she did. In a complete U-turn, she accused Edward and Agnes Bayntun of paying her to say what she had and hence cleared Henry and Dorothy and, of course, Agnes Mylles who had unfortunately already been hanged as a witch. Once free from Sarum prison, Jane Marsh then denied her denial, saying that her original statement had been true all along and she had only denied it in order to gain her freedom.

Centuries later we are left with a complete mystery. Now we are not even sure who, if anybody, was murdered. Was the infant William murdered by witchcraft or was he simply the sad victim of a natural child mortality? If he died from natural causes, then Agnes Mylles had been hanged for a crime she had not committed and therefore those who plotted her downfall must be guilty of murder. Had Jane Marsh been paid to accuse Agnes Mylles? If so, the person who held the purse strings must be implicated along with Jane Marsh. So there must be at least one murder victim, but we don't know which, and indeed possibly we have two murder victims.

What an unnecessary tragedy it all turned out to be. After the death of their first-born child, Agnes went on to produce a further twelve children and the possible inheritance by the step-brother became a virtual impossibility. However, of those thirteen children born of the marriage, only three survived to adulthood, adding weight to the probability that the death of their first-born had been from natural causes after all.

THE MURDER CASE
WITHOUT A BODY

———————❀———————

One of Wiltshire's most interesting murder cases is also one of the most recent and it is just possible that the apparent victim may still be alive. If that is the case, then an innocent man is languishing in Her Majesty's Prison Gartree in Leicestershire, serving a life sentence.

It was 1979 when Glyn Razzell, aged 20, first met 19-year-old Linda Davies on a train. Five years later they married but, despite being blessed with four children, it was not a happy relationship. Glyn Razzell's career developed quite successfully. He had become an insurance investment manager, but in contrast his wife's life appeared to be going nowhere, perhaps overshadowed by his success. With four children at home, Glyn designed an extension to their property and when the builders commenced work, a relationship began between Linda and one of the workmen.

By the summer of 2000, Linda had entered a relationship with the husband of one of her friends and Glyn Razzell had become friendly with a work colleague, Rachel Smith, a lady 20 years younger than himself. They had first met the previous year and initially were simply work colleagues who got on well together, but the relationship reached the level of comfort where Razzell felt he could confide in Rachel regarding the difficulties he was experiencing at home, especially after his discovery of the relationship with the builder and the subsequent affair with her friend's husband.

As the marriage headed towards divorce, amidst acrimonious disagreements over custody of the children, Glyn moved out of the matrimonial home and into a rented property in Swindon.

Linda by now had accused her husband of having twice assaulted her. Glyn Razzell was charged on both occasions and cleared. During their marriage she had been treated on at least two occasions for mental illnesses. That same year, Linda began working part time at Swindon College as a learning support assistant and at the end of the year Glyn Razzell was made redundant from the finance company which employed him. With the redundancy, the maintenance payments to Linda stopped going through.

On Friday, 15 March, Linda obtained a court order to freeze her husband's bank account. On the Monday following, Glyn Razzell's solicitor advised him to get back into court as fast as he could. And that advice is very relevant to what happened next. That same day, Linda Razzell visited three banks in Swindon, supposedly to withdraw money, and amongst her list of things to do was 'Collect travel tickets'. This particular point was never taken up at the subsequent trial.

Glyn had planned to take a trip the following day, the Tuesday, to France with a group of friends. However, with the change of circumstances he pulled out of the trip, but swapped cars with another member of the group. Glyn's car was a large Ford Galaxy and big enough to bring back the wine and cheese which justified the trip. His friend's car, a Renault Laguna, lacked the required capacity and so the swap was agreed.

We come to the critical day, Tuesday, 19 March. The calendar in Linda's house had a question mark against the 19th. At 8.40 am Linda left home at Highworth, near Swindon. Everything was normal except that she left behind her college identity badge. Was this a momentary lapse of concentration or was she in fact not planning to go to work that day? Having dropped off her current partner, she took her children to their respective schools, and then drove into Swindon centre where she parked her car in Alveston Road and disappeared.

Later her mobile phone was found in an alleyway leading into Upham Road, between the car park and the college. Was it dropped there during a struggle in which Linda was abducted? The alleyway is overlooked by a number of houses and it was a busy time of the morning. No one heard any signs of a struggle. From the alleyway, a further walk via Drove Road and Queen's Park, where an underwater search was later to be held, would have brought Linda to the college.

In the early evening, Linda's new partner received a phone call from the Razzells' oldest child to say that their mother had failed to pick up the two youngest children from their school. The police were notified and their enquiries commenced.

Exactly where Glyn Razzell had been during that day remains a matter of speculation. It is known that he visited his solicitor in the town centre. In the early evening, Razzell and Rachel Smith had a meal at the Red Lion in Avebury. Later that same evening, Razzell's friends returned from their trip to France, the goods were shared out and Razzell's Galaxy was returned to him in exchange for the Laguna. From the Monday afternoon to the Tuesday evening, the Galaxy had been in someone else's possession.

Suspicion as to the cause of Linda's disappearance began to fall on Glyn Razzell. The following day, Wednesday, the police spent almost three quarters of an hour checking Razzell's car looking for clues as to his estranged wife's disappearance. They found nothing.

In similar fashion, the Laguna was also checked. The following day, the police returned and this time took the Laguna away and kept it for the following four days. It was given a thorough examination using forensic tests to look for traces of anything that may have provided a lead. Again nothing was found, including, significantly, no indications of the car having been cleaned which may have destroyed any evidence. Eventually the car was returned and, being covered in fingerprint dust, the owner gave it a thorough cleaning during which he saw no signs of blood. A week passed by and the police returned again to collect the Laguna for further tests. Incredibly, this time they found bloodspots, the DNA of which matched that of the missing woman. Her blood was found on the underside of the parcel shelf, on the top of the rear seat, on the mat in the passenger's foot well and on the inside of the boot. Some of these spots were even visible to the naked eye. How could so much evidence have been missed, not once but twice? How in four days of holding the car for forensic examination, could bloodstains visible to the human eye have been overlooked? Equally challenging, despite the presence of bloodstains, there was a complete absence of hair or clothing fibre to match Linda Razzell. There were also DNA samples found from other people, possibly including the murderer if Linda had been murdered and not by Glyn Razzell.

This leaves a huge question mark over the forensic evidence and leaves us with two options. Either the evidence was always there and on two separate occasions the police examinations were carried out incompetently or inadequately. Or the evidence was added after the event by Linda Razzell herself or by some other person with access to her, whether she was alive or dead, in order to incriminate Glyn Razzell.

The second option raises the possibility that Linda Razzell either is not dead, and has simply disappeared by choice and with the intention of making life as difficult as possible for her estranged husband, or she is dead and her real killer planted the evidence.

Let's return to the assumption that Linda Razzell had been abducted on her way to work. There is evidence that at 8.24 am Rachel Smith called Glyn Razzell when she arrived at her office and he was still at home. After that phone call, Razzell went for a two and a half hour walk. It was a journey which took him past the Westlea police station with its CCTV cameras recording everything that happens outside. Those cameras should have provided the evidence of Razzell's presence outside the police station at a time which clearly would not give him the chance to get to where Linda Razzell had parked and to abduct her before she entered her workplace. Inconveniently for Razzell, conveniently for the prosecution in the forthcoming trial, the police declared that the cameras were not working at the very time they were most needed.

As far as motive went, it was assumed that the imminent divorce settlement would have granted Linda Razzell her share of the property and assets from the marriage. Therein lay a possible financial motive. As far as opportunity goes, Glyn Razzell's alibi for his whereabouts at the time of the disappearance lacked concrete evidence. The park in which Razzell claimed to have taken a two and a half hour walk had been visited at the same time by a school party supervised by a number of adults. They all confirmed that none of them could remember seeing him there. CCTV footage from the day of the disappearance showed Glyn Razzell wearing clothes which were not the same as those that he previously claimed he had been wearing on that day. When questioned on this, he said it was just a mistake. Video footage showed him at a petrol station at 7.50 am putting petrol into the Laguna.

If Linda had chosen to disappear, she had left her passport behind. Since her disappearance, there had been no financial withdrawals using her credit or bank cards. There was nothing to indicate that she was still alive. However, a woman who knew Linda Razzell claims to have seen her the day after she disappeared driving what appeared to be someone else's car. There were also apparent sightings of her in Weston-super-Mare and Pendine Sands.

In October 2003, the trial began at Bristol Crown Court. On the final day, the jury of seven men and five women returned their unanimous verdict of guilty of murder. Razzell continues to declare his innocence and Rachel Smith continues to use every spare moment endeavouring to overturn the verdict. Rachel is reported to believe that Linda managed her own disappearance and that at the time of the incident Linda had been reading *Trial and Retribution 3*, a story based in part on the use of evidence planted deliberately to incriminate an innocent person.

Linda Razzell

ENTER THE DRAGON

––––––––––––– ❁ –––––––––––––

Wiltshire is full of mysteries with its UFOs, crop circles and ley lines yet I still find it somewhat amazing that the county can boast the presence of the tallest man-made mound in Europe and yet have no idea why it is there.

Silbury Hill lies in the Winterbourne-Kennet valley between Devizes and Marlborough, about a mile south of Avebury Henge. It has been there for between four and five thousand years. It stands 130 feet high, covering five and a half acres. It is a giant of a construction which must have required a project of military proportions to achieve its completion in those days well before mechanisation. One estimate puts the man-power required at 7,500 man years, assuming they worked six days a week with no holidays. This also assumes that none of them were allowed time off to plant and harvest or to hunt. So there must also have been another huge number of people in support of the work force. Roughly three quarters of the material used in its construction had to be quarried using crude tools made from wood, bone or stone. That material then had to be carried to the site of the hill.

Such an undertaking would clearly require a stable and substantial community over a period of perhaps 30 or 40 years. A community large enough to meet the demands for this major construction would surely have left considerable archaeological traces as to their prolonged presence but there is nothing to find. There is evidence of the hill being used as a defensive position against the marauding Vikings about a thousand years ago, and there is evidence of medieval presence later than that, but nothing of the Neolithic period in which it was built.

What can be the purpose of such a construction? Mounds in their various forms, barrows in particular, are typically burial sites. In many ways, it is like a western version of a pyramid. Yet no grave has ever been found at the site, not even part of a human skeleton. Nor have there been any significant artefacts discovered to point to its purpose. If it was intended as a grave, it must have been the result of an enormous ego trip by some Neolithic chieftain who then failed to benefit from its presence. Perhaps such a chieftain was defeated in battle or overthrown by some tribal internal insurrection and hence failed to receive the hero's funeral he had planned. Perhaps the community simply moved on as one culture clashed with another.

The geographic position of Silbury Hill is significant and in turn could suggest a purpose as a burial mound or equally a defensive position for the numerous other sites at the heart

Silbury Hill

of which it is found. The Avebury Henge, the Sanctuary, the two Avenues, the East and West Kennet long barrows all appear to position themselves geographically around Silbury Hill.

What we do know is that it was created in three distinct phases. The initial phase created a mound which was 20 feet high and five and a half acres in area. It appears that after its construction started, there was a change of plan and the base was enlarged. In the second phase, the size of the hill tripled. At each stage, the mound was capped with chalk which was packed down and smoothed off. The chalk was excavated from ditches 25 feet deep and which run around the base of the hill. The final phase appears to have consisted of six concentric terraces, each level being started with chalk, overlaid with chalk rubble, pieces of flint and gravel, and then the top level mound was cone-shaped with a flat top some hundred feet across, built from earth and covered in turf. With the exception of the final terrace, the distinct terrace shaped of each layer was disguised by adding further soil. In fact recent archaeological exercises taking advantage of modern technologies have discovered that the hill is not so much terraced as spiralled. Viewed from one side of the hill, it appears to be terraced but if you walk around the top terrace, when you return to your start point, you are several feet lower.

There have been three major, and a number of minor, attempts to learn more about the hill, each involving excavation. In 1776 the Duke of Northumberland recruited a team of Cornish miners and they sunk a shaft from top to bottom. In 1849, a tunnel was dug from the edge right into the centre. The miners had to dig for almost a hundred feet through solid chalk until soil was found. In 1867, the Wiltshire Archaeological Society excavated the mound to see if the old Roman road, now the A4, went through it. The present line of the road would pass straight through the hill if it didn't take a detour around it. This provides further evidence of long straight tracks being established as travelling routes long before the arrival of the Romans who simply upgraded them.

In 1886, ten exploratory pits were dug into the surrounding ditch. About eight feet down the explorers hit the water table level. The ditch in its original form was probably about 18 feet deep. Then in 1968, a professor Richard Atkinson oversaw the excavation of a tunnel part way into the base of the hill. The results of these excavations are that we now know what is in the centre of the hill; clay and flints, moss and turf, gravel, freshwater shells, various trees, ox bones and antler tines.

Silbury Hill lies at the crossroads of a number of ancient ley lines, travellers' paths. Its construction could simply have been as a landmark in an area of low lying flattish land, but approaching from almost any direction it does not stand out significantly above the horizon until you are almost upon it. The problem is that it lies in a dip. If you were building a landmark, you wouldn't place it in a dip unless it was a pond you were constructing.

Local legends suggest it is the burial place of King Sil, a long forgotten king who was buried in his golden armour and mounted on a golden horse. Another legend blames its presence on the devil who was so angered by the religious devoutness of the people of Avebury that he decided to bury them under a huge volume of soil. But the observant priests of Avebury saw him coming and cast spells on him such that he was unable to fulfil his mission, and dropped the complete load where Silbury Hill now stands.

Among the slightly more credible explanations is that it was constructed to provide a giant sundial in order to accurately determine the length of the year. This is not as ludicrous as many would believe. Consider the sophistication of Stonehenge and the alignment of its stones to coincide with the sun at key points in the calendar such as the periods of equinox. The people who constructed Silbury Hill and Stonehenge were clearly far more advanced than perhaps we give them credit for. They were a religious people who studied the seasons and the movement of the sun and moon. The prospect of Silbury Hill being part of their research into the accurate length of the calendar year is just plausible.

Enter the Dragon. Similar to our ley lines mentioned in an earlier chapter, in China there are lines which run across the earth called *Lung Mei*, the paths of the dragon. The ancient Chinese believed that these paths covered the whole earth. Along such paths they built mounds for astronomical sightings and erected stones to mark the path of the dragon. They believed that when the dragon was allowed to run long distances in a straight line, it would build up dangerous levels of energy. Therefore along the lines, barriers were erected, such as standing stones or earth mounds. These helped to diffuse the energy from the dragon which dissipated into the stones or mound, which then contained useful energy. It is from this belief that Feng Shui is derived.

Now this may all seem very fanciful and it hardly matters if you believe in the power of Feng Shui or not. What matters is that you understand that the ancient Chinese believed it. If you can accept that, and if you can see the parallels between the Chinese dragon lines and the ley lines which run through Wiltshire, then perhaps therein lies the explanation for the presence of Silbury Hill. If between four and five thousand years ago, there were similar beliefs across the two nations mentioned, in respect of ley lines and dragon lines, that along those ancient routes of travel, barriers and markers had to be created, whether in Wiltshire or China, then we can understand why a mound having no other apparent purpose could be built at the conjunction of so many ancient straight tracks.

And what an amazing coincidence that Silbury Hill lies on the St Michael ley line which starts at St Michael's Mount in Cornwall and continues in a straight line across the full width of England, and passes through so many 'St Michael' churches on its way. Then consider how St Michael for thousands of years has been universally recognised as the slayer of dragons, and perhaps we have the answer to why Silbury Hill was constructed.

Acknowledgements

Carol Date; Dot Gulliver (John Gurd murders); Angharad Little (Murder of Ann Little); Ann Hamilton (Zoë Evans's grandmother); Craig Evry (*Wiltshire Times*); Paul Wilkinson (Highwayman illustration); Michael Stirling (Edington Enigma); Rachel Smith (Linda Razzell illustration); Bernadette Siebert and Megan Thompson (Stephen Rodway murder).

Bibliography

Bristol Mercury and Daily Post, (October 12, 1889). "Witchcraft in Wiltshire." *Northern Daily Telegraph* (Blackburn, England), October 8, 1889, p.2 c.6.

The Newgate Calendar Improved (pub. George Wilkinson) 1816.

The Old Straight Tracks of Wessex; Paul Devereux and Laurence Main, Cheltenham; Thornhill Press, 1992

The Old Straight Track, Alfred Watkins, London, Abacus, 1997

The Somerset Moors; Part 2 The Battle of Edington; Michael Stirling, Middlezoy, Michael Stirling, 2002